My Lowest

His Highest

KAT SHULTIS

My Lowest

FOR

His Highest

Fixing Our Eyes on Jesus
in the Midst of Broken Dreams

MOODY PUBLISHERS
CHICAGO

Edited by Ashleigh Slater
Interior and cover design: Kaylee Dunn
Cover graphic of butterfly copyright © 2023 by dariaustiugova/Adobe Stock (360928293). All rights reserved.
Cover graphic of birth of a butterfly copyright © 2023 by dariaustiugova/Adobe Stock (360928286). All rights reserved.

Library of Congress Cataloging-in-Publication Data

Names: Shultis, Kathryn, author.
Title: My lowest for his highest : fixing our eyes on Jesus in
   the midst of broken dreams / by Kathryn Shultis.
Description: 1st. | Chicago, IL : Moody Publishers, 2024. | Includes
   bibliographical references. | Summary: "How do you walk through hard
   seasons of disappointment and learn to heal? You will find your heart
   strengthened and encouraged as you travel with Kathryn-through her
   triumphs and failures-and discover the hope of persevering in the love
   and power of Jesus"-- Provided by publisher.
Identifiers: LCCN 2023040493 | ISBN 9780802429575 (paperback) | ISBN
   9780802473530 (ebook)
Subjects: LCSH: Christian life. | Healing--Religious aspects--Chrisitanity.
   | Disappointment--Religious aspects--Christianity. | BISAC: RELIGION /
   Christian Living / Women's Interests | RELIGION / Christian Living /
   Personal Memoirs
Classification: LCC BV4501.3 .S5754 2024 | DDC 248.4--dc23/eng/20231102
LC record available at https://lccn.loc.gov/2023040493

Originally delivered by fleets of horse-drawn wagons, the affordable paperbacks from D. L. Moody's publishing house resourced the church and served everyday people. Now, after more than 125 years of publishing and ministry, Moody Publishers' mission remains the same—even if our delivery systems have changed a bit. For more information on other books (and resources) created from a biblical perspective, go to www.moodypublishers.com or write to:

Moody Publishers
820 N. LaSalle Boulevard
Chicago, IL 60610

1 3 5 7 9 10 8 6 4 2

Printed in the United States of America

To my dad, thank you for teaching me what it is like to love Jesus with your whole heart. To my role models, thank you for helping me never give up. To my Casey boy, thank you for cheering on my dreams even more than you do your own. To my sweet Jesus, thank you for being the closest friend on the darkest of days.

Contents

1

A Father's Love

One crisp, cool October afternoon about eight years ago, I was getting home from a doctor's appointment. As my dad and I rolled up to our new home in Douglasville, Georgia, I was doing my best to hold the tears in until I could get to my room to be alone.

While at the doctor's office, we had gotten bad news about a running injury I was dealing with. Almost a year before, I had just finished up my dream cross-country season, which I ended having qualified for nationals as one of the top high school sophomores in the nation. I was now at this specialist because when I had started running again after a two-week break, I had a bad fall on my first run back. I ended up severely injuring my foot and still had some lingering hip issues as I had landed on it. Turns out I had torn the labral cartilage in my hip socket.

To say the least, the doctor had not done a very good job of encouraging me. I was in the middle of another cross-country season and was not able to run due to a lot of lower back and hip pain that had been ongoing since the accident. He had been very clear that this pain would most likely never go away or heal due to the shape of my spine from scoliosis.

Within a matter of seconds of entering the house, I was upstairs in my closet crying. You know those deep sobs where you can hardly cry because you are so upset? It is not as loud as normal crying, but it is deeper, harder, and more passionate.

I had finished last fall with the realization that I would get to run anywhere I wanted in college. Based on my national ranking, time for my age, and performance, it was looking like there was a large chance I would go pro and be a runner for my dream job someday. But now I was ten months out from this damaging fall, and nothing had gone my way since that moment of pain on the ground.

I had not been the same runner and had experienced nothing but health issues and doctor visits for almost a year. It felt like I was at the end of my rope, waiting for answers to help me get back to my dream of running. I sat in the closet crying, asking God to explain, just wanting to go back to the way my life was before.

My dad heard me from downstairs. Shortly after, there was a soft *tap, tap* on my bedroom door. I got up to answer, and as soon as I saw my dad's face, I burst into another fit of tears. I could see in his eyes the empathy and pain he felt. He came and sat with me in my closet and let me have a good, long cry.

"Why me?" I asked him. "Why do I have to go through this when none of my friends do?"

My dad held me and rubbed my back as the long, deep sobs turned into a snotty nose and slow tears running down my face. He answered in a slow, apologetic voice, almost on the edge of tears himself. He told me he did not know why I had to go through this. He said he wished I did not have to.

Then, he began to slowly unpack the story of Lazarus in the Bible for me. He said, "I don't know why, but this is what God does to His friends. All throughout the Bible, He does *this* to His closest friends."

GET BACK UP

This past fall, I spoke at a small women's conference about the story of Lazarus. I encouraged the women listening to see Jesus' empathy for Lazarus as an example of how He cares for us in the pain we face in life. (Before I share more, I want to be clear that I do not mean God wishes evil upon us. But I do believe that whatever pain we walk through in life, God is able to use.)

Before speaking at this event, I reread the passages in John 11 over and over to study exactly what Jesus did in this story of Lazarus. I wanted to make sure I said everything in the right context and shared the heart of God with these women through this moving story. About my third time reading through it, I remember being so powerfully moved by these four verses:

> Now when Mary came to where Jesus was and saw him, she fell at his feet, saying to him, "Lord, if you had been here, my brother would not have died." When Jesus saw her weeping, and the Jews who had come with her also weeping, he was deeply moved in his spirit and greatly troubled. And he said, "Where have you laid him?" They said to him, "Lord, come and see." Jesus wept. (John 11:32–35)

Now, in the verses before this, John talks about when Jesus first got the news that Lazarus was sick. John states that Jesus was good friends with Lazarus and his sisters, Mary and Martha. These women are two significant people in the Bible and loved the Lord intimately just as He loved them. But John also tells us that Jesus waited two days before going to Judea to see Lazarus. Imagine knowing you had the power to help a close friend or relative who was on death's doorstep, and you had to let them pass and wait two days before going to check on their family.

I think the most significant verse in this story is verse 35—the shortest verse in the Bible—"Jesus wept." You might think, yes, Lazarus was His close friend. Of course, Jesus cried. But to me, the crazy beautiful part of Jesus being "deeply moved" by Mary's and Martha's tears, as it says in verse 33, is that Jesus knew He was about to go raise Lazarus from the dead. Even though Lazarus had been dead four days, Jesus knew He had the power to heal him and had told His disciples verses before, "Our friend Lazarus has fallen asleep, but I go to awaken him" (John 11:11). Jesus knew what He came to Judea to do. He could have come in dancing and praising and joyful because He knew He was about to bring glory to God, but He didn't.

Instead, Jesus hurt with them. He physically wept with them. And then He said, "Where have you laid him?" (John 11:34). After Lazarus was raised, much glory was brought to God, and many believed. But that did not change the fact that the pain of Lazarus and his family was intense. There had been death and tears.

If you just opened this book and you are not sure if it is for you but reading this story about Lazarus reminded you a bit of your own story, I encourage you to keep reading. Friend, God *loves you*, with a capital L. However, sometimes things in our lives have to die before He can raise up something beautiful. When this happens, our most helpful response is, "Lord, come." I've learned we have to ask Him to come and be with us in the brokenness that we do not understand.

Jesus hates to see us hurt, but He loves us so much that when we feel pain, He feels it with and for us. How significant a love our God has that He does not simply show up celebrating because He knows the end of the story. He knows the final outcome is good, but He still holds us and allows us to lean back against His chest and feel His heartbeat. He knows how to love us better than anyone.

ENVIABLE INTIMACY

My husband, Casey, and I have been reading The Chronicles of Narnia by C. S. Lewis aloud to each other anytime we are on a long road trip or getting ready to go to bed. We try to read instead of being on our phones all the time. If you have not read the Narnia stories, I will give you a little context. In the series, Aslan represents God, and he is a lion.

We were reading *The Magician's Nephew* a few weeks ago. It parallels the creation story in the Bible. Digory, the main character, is a child who has a very sick mother. He realizes Aslan might heal her as he gets to know how powerful and kind Aslan is.

I couldn't hold back my tears when I read the following passage aloud:

> "But please, please—won't you—can't you give me something that will cure Mother?" Up till then he had been looking at the Lion's great feet and the huge claws on them; now, in his despair, he looked up at its face. What he saw surprised him as much as anything in his whole life. For the tawny face was bent down near his own and (wonder of wonders) great shining tears stood in the Lion's eyes. They were such big, bright tears compared with Digory's own that for a moment he felt as if the Lion must really be sorrier about his Mother than he was himself.[1]

I don't claim to know why God does what He does or why He allows certain things to happen to us. But the truth is, as my dad shared with me after that disappointing doctor's appointment, Jesus' "best friends"—those who have enviable intimacy with Him—almost always have hard stories because that's how that intimacy grows. Just think back to Lazarus and his sisters, Mary and Martha.

We also see this in so many of those closest to God throughout Scripture. Job had his whole life stripped from him but still trusted God's goodness when everyone told him to give up (Job 1:20–21). David went through massive hardships before he ever became king, as God promised and called him to (Ps. 13:1–6). Abraham and Sarah went through decades of infertility before receiving the son God promised them (Gen. 21:1–3). The list goes on and on.

Like those in the Bible, we do not have to know why God allows us to break. We just have to know He does not leave us that way. We can draw closer to Him by fighting battles with Him and for Him.

The circumstances of this life cannot be what defines my joy or yours. Running fast and being injury-free was never supposed to be my purpose. Being "skinny," "fit," or "having goals" were not meant to be my purpose either. I can see now that God was using every hard "closet moment" with Him to help me develop a sense of identity, purpose, and love for Him far beyond what I already had. And every time you and I look into God's eyes, just as Mary did after her brother Lazarus died, just like Digory did when he thought about his mother being sick and possibly dying, we get to see God's character. And His character is love, empathy, goodness.

I wanted to set the tone of this book right off the bat in this first chapter by letting you know God loves you—and, as I said earlier, it's with a capital L. You are probably thinking, *Okay, Kat, I have heard that a million times, I know. I do not need another book on that.* I think as believers we do *know* God loves us because we hear it so often. But I think sometimes we forget that loving someone can involve pain. For some of us, when we walk through painful seasons—full of death or sickness, broken dreams, or a broken heart—it is hard to not become numb to the love of God.

I remember when I hit the peak of all my injuries and disappointment over running. It was a few years after that first fall when I tore my hip. I was in college, depressed and convinced I would never feel like myself again, and dealing with an eating disorder. After years of rehab to get the previous tear to an okay state to where I could run, I tore the hip cartilage on my good leg. It truly just felt like everything was wrong and life would not be right again.

I was going to church and hearing messages talking about trusting God. The pastors were saying things like, "Everything is going to be okay," and I felt so much resentment toward them for saying these clichéd things I had heard so many times. They felt so untrue in my current circumstances. I never had a "rebellious" phase where I fell away from God. I always loved Him and believed. But I did struggle for years before I felt like I could trust Him during pain. I knew the words, "He is good," but I did not know deep down for myself that even in the midst of the pain it could be good.

WHERE LOVE IS MORE PRECIOUS
THAN A PAIN-FREE LIFE

A while back, I had a girl direct message me on social media. I had no idea who she was, but she said God put it on her heart to send me a book called *Hinds' Feet on High Places*. She described how the book talks a lot about my life verse, Isaiah 52:7. I had talked about this verse in my posts, so that is how she knew what it meant to me.

I looked through her page and she seemed trustworthy. I had peace about giving her my address (which is not something I would normally do), and thanked her for sending me the book. I received it along with a sweet note and glanced at a few pages, but failed to read it until years later. Once I did pick it up, it was evident this was a resource God meant for me to have in my hand.

Hannah Hurnard, the author of *Hinds' Feet on High Places*, talks about a girl named Much-Afraid, who lives in the Valley of Fear and is tormented by her fearful and taunting relatives. It is a very *Pilgrim's Progress*–style read where the Good Shepherd begins to walk Much-Afraid out of her captive mindset. He shows her that with His help she can walk through hard things and get to the Valley of Love where His Father reigns.

Like me, Much-Afraid struggles intensely with a fear of pain. I struggled with a triggering fear of pain for years because of the trauma from all of my injuries, doctors' appointments, broken dreams, and depression. Even today, whenever I feel a twinge of pain in my right hip, where my first labral tear occurred, I start to worry and think about the worst-case scenario. That physical sense of pain still makes me feel shame about my body because it triggers an emotional response in me from all of the disordered eating thoughts and body image issues I walked through during my hip tears and injuries in high school and college. (I'll talk more about this in later chapters.) It is wild how much of a marker pain can leave on our lives.

I think in some ways, we are all wired like this. The enemy is so good at lying to us, and I've discovered pain is one of his top ways to do so. He loves to tell us, "It will always be this way. You can never beat this. Remember how bad that hurt you? God is going to allow it to happen again." It is hard not to fall into believing these lies because the enemy is good at what he does. His name is "the deceiver" (Rev. 12:9).

The only true defense mechanism I have found against these lies is my Father's heart. The more time I spend on my phone or in my busy world where temptation and depression run rampant, the less in tune I feel with God and His truth. However, the more time I spend with my Father, getting to know His heart, and leaning into His presence in my prayer closet, the closer I am to the truth and the easier it is to detect a lie and dismiss it. When we fall in love with the Lord, we are saying, "I trust You." We are choosing to believe what Paul wrote when he said, "For I consider that the sufferings of this present time are not worth comparing to the glory that is to be revealed to us" (Rom. 8:18).

In Hurnard's *Hinds' Feet*, there is a leap-of-faith moment where the Good Shepherd—who represents *abba* (the Aramaic word for *father*)—says:

"To love does mean to put yourself into the power of the loved one and to become very vulnerable to pain, and you are very Much-Afraid of pain, are you not? . . . But it is so happy to love. . . . It is happy to love even if you are not loved in return. There is pain too, certainly, but Love does not think that very significant."[2]

Jesus going to the cross and His Father allowing Him to die hurt deeply. This hurt shows us that love is more significant than pain. The Father loved His Son and He loved us so much that He allowed Jesus to go through the most painful act of all so that we might be saved. What a glorious gift we daily take for granted!

But how do we get to this state where love is more precious than living a pain-free life? How can we have this kind of surrender and sacrifice? For me, it happened in waves. One of these first waves was on a rainy summer night a few years back.

WHEN WE WORSHIP

One rainy August night, back in high school, I was driving home from our local Starbucks where I had been catching up on some homework and having my daily time with the Lord. I was playing worship music, and our neighborhood had a very long street with a lot of speed bumps, so it took me a good song or two just to get home once I entered the neighborhood.

As I drove onto the familiar road I had taken home every day for the past few years, a new song by Lauren Daigle came on called "I Am Yours." She was my favorite artist at the time, and, with all I was walking through in the realms of pain and disappointment, I related heavily to the deep cry of her lyrics.

I had hit my third season in a row with a new injury nagging me and was seeing many doctors a week for some unexplained health issues outside of just the injuries. My body was failing me, so I felt like a failure even though I was working harder than I ever had to try and get healthy and happy again. It felt like all of my dreams for the future and running and who I thought I was were crashing to the ground. Lauren's lyrics helped remind me that God was trustworthy even when not much else in life felt good.

I had been battling the surrender of my will. My desire for my running dreams to come true was stronger than my desire for trusting God. But driving home in the rain that day, screaming Lauren's lyrics in surrender, something clicked.

God was walking me through something deeply painful, but I just kept asking Him for a pain-free life. I sat in the car weeping and screaming the lyrics to this song, asking God to help my love for Him be stronger than my current circumstances. I knew full well that I was asking God for more trials if that was what He willed, but trust was truly clicking for one of the first times in my life. I was realizing that, yes, I didn't want the hard things, but I wanted more of God's presence and will in my life than anything else. So I asked Him for the first time in years to lead me where I fully trusted Him and I would not walk on my own.

The realization of what I had just done was hard because I knew trusting Him like that might be surprisingly harder than I expected. And from the past few years of disappointing surprises, I had grown to dread hard things. I was scared to say, "I trust You, God. Your will be done," because in the past when His will was done, it hurt. I felt scared that I might not like whatever God wanted to do with my life. I had come to believe that all of the hard health issues and things I had gone through over the years were not worth anything and were just wasted years and potential. It was very easy for me to become a pessimist when I listened to the enemy's lies in my life.

Since that day, I have learned and experienced deeper levels of God's goodness, His kindness, and His love. God was always doing something in my life; I just had to trust Him enough to stay with Him during the storms. To know Him is to love Him. I am praying you can enter into this kind of love as you read this book. We will have empathy with one another as we discuss pain and disappointment, but more importantly, we will accept the truth that sets us free.

EVERY MOMENT

Before we wrap up this chapter, I want to speak to the girl who has enjoyed the start of the book but still doesn't know if it is "for her." The girl who is not walking through something difficult at this moment, but has in her past and has some scars she does not consider beautiful yet. I understand. I've been there too. We may love our Father now and be great at surrendering our current circumstances to Him, but how do we hand Him those ugly parts of us we do not tell anyone else about? How do we consider the ugliness of our past beautiful? How do we trust He was doing something all along? I want to share one more story for that girl and all of us.

During my freshman year at Baylor University in Waco, Texas, I spent most of my time cross-training instead of running after I tore the cartilage on my second hip and struggled with injuries for another year. I remember going to a small church basement with a small aquatic center-style pool for their members to do water aerobics and therapy exercises.

Every morning at 5 a.m., you could find me swimming either by myself or with a few older people doing water aerobics. I would stare at the old-school clock on the wall, waiting desperately for my one to two hours of solitude and water jogging to be over. I hated those lonesome hours. I would tread water around the whole pool and then stare up at the clock to see if I had gotten through another five minutes yet. I would play worship music from the side of the pool on my phone to get me through the lonely hours. Lauren Daigle was still one of my favorites.

During the past month or so, I have been worshiping to Upper Room music on YouTube quite frequently. One of their recent music videos is called "Hey, Jesus." Some of the lyrics talk about how Jesus was there every single moment, and when we look back, we can see He was there. The image they used with these lyrics is an old-school clock.

Anytime I see an old-school clock, I am still reminded of that lonely pool in Waco. So I burst into tears the first time I saw it with the song lyrics plastered over it in the worship video. God reminded me that He had seen every moment of pain. And not just seen the pain but had been there with me in it. Every moment of loneliness at 5 a.m., as I drove myself to the cold pool, He was in the car with me. When no other teammate, friend, or family member was there, He was.

I encourage you to look back on your loneliest and hardest moments. How do you see God was there? Have you convinced yourself He was not? If so, I encourage you to look harder. Sometimes, I think it can be frowned upon when we see God in everything. People make fun of us or think we are "over-spiritual." But friend, who cares what others think because God made everything and *is* truly in everything.

When I was little, my father used to tell me to look out the window when the wind was blowing the trees hard. He would say, "Look how even the trees praise Him. How much more so should we." As we move through this book together and talk through pain and disappointment, I encourage us to see it as an opportunity to grow in our intimacy with God and proclaim He is good above it all! To commit our lowest to His highest.

Even when it seems cliché to sing the same song lyrics again, will you? Even when it does not ring true in your circumstances, will you believe beyond that? The enemy says to dwell in our self-pity and remain navel-gazing instead of getting into our Father's arms. I pray I make the decision to see God for who and where He is and that you will join me.

I hope we make space for Jesus to come into our corner, just like my dad came into my closet after that discouraging doctor's appointment. I left that moment with my dad, proud and determined instead of desperate and at the end of my rope. When we meet with God, He ministers to us, picks us up, and reminds us that He is a good Father.

2

When a Dream Gets Broken

Throughout high school, I loved dreaming with God. I loved dreaming about the things I would accomplish someday for and with Him. You know when you are a little kid and everyone is like, "So, what do you want to be when you grow up?" When I was little my answer was always, "A mom. I want to be a really good mom." As soon as I was sixth in the nation in cross country in eighth grade, that changed to, "An Olympian. I want to go to the Olympics." We all have dreams or ideas of what we want to accomplish. As certain things change in our lives, we get better at homing in on exactly what our God-sized dreams should be. We learn to ask God what He desires for us and what we should be working toward with Him. For me, the path was clear in early high school: God made me good at running.

Growing up, my parents read my siblings and me missionary books a lot. The series my mom always read to us from was called Christian Heroes: Then and Now. It is a series by YWAM Publishing with many different detailed stories of missionary heroes. The covers of the books are all brown and gold with pictures or symbols from whatever country the missionary was in.

I recently looked up one of the books on Audible to listen to it again, and seeing the cover made me think of warm memories sitting around the fire with my parents listening to my mom read intense, thrilling, sacrificial, and motivational stories about Christian heroes. Hearing their stories instilled in me at a young age the desire to be tried for the gospel. I did not want to be a hero as the world saw it, but a hero in the eyes of Jesus for the kingdom of heaven.

There was one of these books I read over and over—Eric Liddell's story. It was called *Something Greater than Gold*[1] and it was the most important to me in the missionary series. There had been a movie made about Eric's life called *Chariots of Fire*. We watched this movie as a tradition before every season's first cross-country or track race. It was boring to some people because it was an old-school movie, but not to me.

Eric's story lit me on fire. My favorite quote from it is fairly well-known. Talking about his running career, Eric always stated that he could feel God's pleasure when he ran. I *knew* this feeling. To be in the midst of a hard race, pushing myself farther and farther into a chilled wind, asking the Lord for strength, knowing He would provide until the finish line. To run, to win, and to know you are doing it for Him. I loved that feeling more than anything. This is why I loved watching *Chariots of Fire*, because I related to it so deeply.

Eric's story is a lot more than just winning races, though. The year after winning his Olympic gold medal, he went to China to do missionary work in the middle of a war, and he started a family. Eric ended up dying a martyr during his missionary work. I strongly encourage you to go read about Eric for yourself, as I do not have the time or word count to do him justice here.

I wanted to inspire people through my dreams like Eric did. I was fast and I felt God's pleasure.

NOT AGAIN

However, my high school junior year cross-country season began and my dreams were quickly shattered when my running got slower and slower, one week at a time. The frustration this time was different because there wasn't one physical pain or injury to blame it on. We found out two years later that I had been very low on a specific vitamin my body needed. My legs simply could not move fast after one mile of racing. I struggled, remaining confused and frustrated. I knew I was faster than most of the people who were beating me because I had beat them by minutes in the past. I knew there was something wrong with me. I just couldn't figure out what it was on my own.

So, doctors and physical therapists became my everyday. In my junior and senior years of high school, I was out of school more than I was in it. My friends expected me to be absent from class because of the doctor, so it was more of a surprise for me to be present in class than to be gone. And after that rare vitamin deficieny, along with strained adductor muscles, torn hips, a scoliosis diagnosis, every other month being in a boot for another tendon or ligament strain, and a myriad of other health issues, I was tired and disappointed to say the least.

One of the hardest parts of the injuries I experienced was going on official visits to see where I would run in college. The other girls on the visits with me were all able to run together. They all seemed healthy, fit, fast, and happy. In the mornings, they would talk about how they were going to run these beautiful trails by rivers and end at the farmer's market where they would get breakfast together. On and on about how dreamy the day would be. But I was not part of those plans. I was stuck in the training room, biking by myself for hours, because I was still hurt. Finding out where I was going to college was hard in the first place, but adding isolation to the process made it even harder.

Injuries quickly put my "national ranking" in the back of college coaches' minds. Instead of being nationally ranked, now I was just another girl trying to get a walk-on spot.

Even if you are not an athlete, all of us have some form of injury. It could be a family issue, a health issue, an eating disorder, a break up, the death of a friend, or a plethora of other things. All our hearts feel handicapped at certain points in our lives from something we go through.

Once I got to Baylor, everything was great for a few months as my physical therapy routine from high school seemed to be working. Right before high school graduation, we had figured out my odd two-year fatigue issue with the sub-level of iron and supplementation fix. After a few months of training hard in Waco with no injuries to hinder me, I was getting close to my old self—the real me! Then, the thing I had spent nights praying and crying wouldn't happen again, happened—I got hurt again. The injury I had struggled with so much in high school was a tear in the right labral tissue of my hip. Now, mid cross-country season at Baylor, there was a tear in my left. I spent hours and hours on the bike and in the training room, getting any and every kind of treatment they could offer, but nothing helped. This kind of tear does not regenerate and could cause pain for the rest of my life.

It felt like everything that the doctor had told me that day back in high school about my spine was true. I had spent three years in physical therapy for the first hip tear, which had continued to nag me and cause other injuries until I finally figured out the perfect routine to keep the pain at bay. Now, here I was with the opposite hip tearing and having to start the whole process over again.

Even though I was not able to train leading up to nationals after I tore my left hip in high school, I did run D1 NCAA Nationals with my team at Baylor in 2016 through intense pain. My coach believed I had earned my spot on the team before the injury occurred. However, on race day, I came in dead last. I limped through the pain the whole time, even though I was on some pretty intense pain meds. The nationally ranked Kathryn Foreman from high school got last place. I got the pity clap! I never in my life would've thought I would be getting the pity clap. "God brings us to our lowest for His highest, right? Or something like that," I told my dad that after the race on that cold, snowy November day.

Weirdly enough, even after quitting collegiate running years later, I still struggle with feeling shame over that race where I came in last—and the shame of not living up to the standard I wanted for my life.

Your "letdown" may not be getting last in a race, but it could be something else. We all have hard experiences in life. Whether it is something massively tragic like someone dying in your family, you simply get the flu, or you fail a test, big or little, bad things happen. It's part of life. Dreams get broken the same as they can come true.

NOT IN THE GARDEN ANYMORE

How do we deal with the things we do not like happening, though? Lysa TerKeurst is one of my favorite authors, and in one of her books, *It's Not Supposed to Be This Way*, she discusses how when bad things happen, we have to know why life is not perfect.[2]

When Adam and Eve sinned, we left the perfect garden. Now we are awaiting heaven, the second place of perfection we will reside. We are in the in-between right now, and though God is with us every step of the way, this imperfect world is not our home. We are running toward heaven together. We are not alone, and it will not be like this forever.

When we understand these realities, we can embrace the truth that those painful places in our lives don't have to be all pain. They don't have to stay dark places. We can light them up.

How do we do this? So far, the painful places have been pretty bad for me, and I have not trusted God and found joy in the journey the way I should. But each day brings new chances to try again, grow a little closer to Jesus, and let Him a little deeper into my heart. As I talked about in chapter 1, trusting Him comes in waves. We slowly but surely realize this hurts, but His love is stronger than the pain. I may be limping, but He will carry me, so it is well with my soul.

Every time I come out of an injury or a hard season, I see the light at the end of the tunnel again, and I am so thankful. But God wants me to be full of hope even if I feel like I'm walking through "the valley of the shadow of death" (Ps. 23:4). Sometimes I still get a little "ouch" in my chest when I think about how much pain I went through with running and how many dreams I saw crash and burn. But through this process, I have learned to make God my number one dream.

Looping back to Eric Liddell's story, he knew all along that there was something greater than gold, and greater than anything he could dream up on his own. So, how do we ask God for more dreams and not sit in fear once a dream has broken?

If you take away anything from this book, hear these words. This is my heart for us that we would understand how to dream with God in the midst of broken dreams. That we would not become bitter. Concerning the surrender of our own ability or dreams, A. W. Tozer says it best:

> Our gifts and talents should also be turned over to Him. They should be recognized for what they are, God's loan to us, and should never be considered in any sense our own. We have no more right to claim credit for special abilities than for blue eyes or strong muscles. "For who maketh thee to differ from another? And what hast thou that thou didst not receive?" (1 Corinthians 4:7).[3]

It is so important for us to use the gifts and talents God gives us for His honor and glory, but at the same time, we cannot hold on to them too tightly because we do not own them. One of my high school track coaches used to always say "palms up" when he was describing how we should live our lives. He said that if your palms are up toward the sky, you are in a position to receive more blessing, but what is in your hand is also available to be taken away if it needs to be. I believe it is this key position of "open surrender" that we miss sometimes. We are fine with the "palms up" mentality when God is blessing us, but as soon as we feel the slightest fear of something being taken away, we close our fists and no longer trust the God who gives and takes away.

We can look at Abraham in the Bible as a great example of how to live "palms up." Genesis 22:1–4 states:

> After these things God tested Abraham and said to him, "Abraham!" And he said, "Here I am." He said, "Take your son, your only son Isaac, whom you love, and go to the

land of Moriah, and offer him there as a burnt offering on
one of the mountains of which I shall tell you." So Abraham rose early in the morning, saddled his donkey, and
took two of his young men with him, and his son Isaac.

If you are not very familiar with the story of Abraham, he
and his wife, Sarah, had waited decades for a son. God had
promised them that He would give them a son even though
they seemed infertile. Imagine believing God for something for
that long, and as soon as you get it, He says, "Give it back to
Me." Our initial selfish reaction is to say, "No, mine." I think
every young child goes through the "No, mine" phase. It is in
our human nature to protect what we believe to be ours.

However, as soon as God asked Abraham to sacrifice, he was
willing. In fact, Scripture says, he went "early in the morning"
(Gen. 22:3). He did not procrastinate. He surrendered and did
as God said right away. When Abraham was about to sacrifice
Isaac, his only son, God sent the angel of the Lord, who told
him to stop. The angel said, "Do not lay your hand on the boy or
do anything to him, for now I know that you fear God, seeing
you have not withheld your son, your only son, from me" (Gen.
22:12). As the passage continues, the Lord speaks through the
angel again, saying:

> "Because you have done this and have not withheld your
> son, your only son, I will surely bless you, and I will surely
> multiply your offspring as the stars of heaven and as the
> sand that is on the seashore. . . . And in your offspring
> shall all the nations of the earth be blessed, because you
> have obeyed my voice." (Gen. 22:16–18)

Describing this passage, A. W. Tozer states, "We must in our hearts live through Abraham's harsh and bitter experiences if we would know the blessedness which follows them."[4]

IT IS OKAY TO LOOK A LITTLE CRAZY

Just like Abraham, sometimes God asks us to do things that look a little crazy to everyone around us. In my junior year of college, I had my first injury-free cross-country season in close to eight years, and I felt God asking me to quit running.

I prayed about it for eight weeks, and when I told certain people I looked up to about my decision, they made me feel insane. One even called me "ludicrous." I definitely had days where I doubted my decision, but I knew I was walking in obedience to the Lord by stepping away from running. But it was hard to hear God's voice over everyone else's. It not only did not make sense to them but hardly made sense to me other than the fact that I knew deep down I was supposed to quit.

Quitting was hard for many other reasons too. The number one reason being I was concerned about how I would pay for college without running. I had transferred to Samford University after my first year at Baylor. Keeping my scholarship and being able to afford my last year and a half at Samford was contingent on being able to run. It was amazing to watch God open door after door with jobs, financial aid, scholarships, and more after I quit.

I remember after one meeting with financial aid, I got approved for enough money to stay at school until I graduated. I walked out of the office in awe. As soon as I got outside, I started to cry and just kept saying, "God, You're so good. God, You're so good. God, You're so good!" I said it over and over in amazement at how God had provided for me after I had made what looked like a stupid decision to the world.

This is what is so cool to me about walking with the Lord. When we decide to truly believe He is good, like He says He is, and trust His plan for us over what we want to happen, it is wild to see how much God is in the details. I won't mention all the doors that opened that spring after quitting because it is a whole other book! But I will ask you to look for those doors in your life. What door has been closed that you keep knocking on? There might be one right next to it that God wants you to knock on instead. I would not have chosen speaking, writing, and social media for myself as dreams because all I wanted to do was run fast in high school and college. I definitely loved God and prayed, worshiped, and ran for His glory, but I did not always do the best job of making His dreams come before my own.

Once Casey and I got married, I started to come to a better understanding of "not my will, but yours" (Luke 22:42). I was struggling intensely with purpose, dreams, jobs, and forms of postgrad depression, some might say. I still needed a new dream since I was not running anymore. I remember the day it clicked for me.

I was walking through Piedmont Park in downtown Atlanta, listening to an episode of Bob Goff's *Dream Big* podcast. I had been listening to pretty much all of Bob's podcasts because the people he interviewed had very cool dreams that came true even though they had odds set against them. In Bob's *Dream Big* book, he discusses the question we often consider when wanting to dream big: *Will our dreams come true, or will they crash and burn?* I was so scared of dreaming again because I had seen all of my ambitions crash and burn in high school and early college. But regarding this fear, Bob states:

We don't know how our lives will turn out, much less whether our ideas are going to work or not. I meet so many people in my travels, good people with great ideas, but many of them never take their ideas out of the hangar. The reason is simple. They're afraid of what they'll do if it works or afraid they'll look bad if it doesn't. . . . It just requires a willingness to fail.[5]

Bob's book and podcast were so pivotal for me at the time because he gave me permission to accept my past crash and burns without an intense dread of history repeating itself.

During that season of feeling so purposeless and relearning how to dream again, I sat down and made a YouTube video on my channel. As a newlywed and recent college graduate, I talked about dreams and purpose and simply told girls like myself, "Listen, all we can do is dream with God. But He has to be our biggest dream the whole time." And now, years later, that is still so true in my life. If we want to live out our God-sized dreams, He has to be the one we treasure above anything!

So, let me give an example. Say I want to write a book to help encourage Christian girls. I have this goal, but first, I am asking God if it is in His will for me to do that. And, if I get a yes, then throughout the entire book writing and publishing process, I have to make sure I am always focused more on God than the book. If I do not wake up and spend time with God, asking Him for wisdom and praying about what my book should be about, then it will not be a very good Christian living book.

It is this way with every aspect of our life. God is our first love, most epic love story, and greatest pursuer. Maybe you hope to get married and have a wonderful husband someday, but if we "worship" the idea of having a husband more than we worship

God, that will put our spouse in the place of God, and that is not healthy. Almost any goal or dream we have can quickly take this seat as god in our life if we are not careful. We have to be excited about what God is allowing us to step into in any season while also having "palms up" the entire time.

I want to end this chapter with a prayer from A. W. Tozer. He acknowledges the deep struggle of the surrender, but focuses on the greater blessing that is Christ having no rival within our hearts. He prays:

> Father, I want to know Thee, but my coward heart fears to give up its toys. I cannot part with them without inward bleeding, and I do not try to hide from Thee the terror of the parting. I come trembling, but I do come. Please root from my heart all those things which I have cherished so long and which have become a very part of my living self, so that Thou mayest enter and dwell there without a rival. Then shalt Thou make the place of Thy feet glorious. Then shall my heart have no need of the sun to shine in it, for Thyself wilt be the light of it, and there shall be no night there. In Jesus' Name, Amen.[6]

When a dream gets broken, we get to tap into what Eric Liddell's running and missionary career so passionately shows—that God's glory is so much greater than any "gold" a flashy dream might hold. When we learn to enjoy and glorify God in any season, whether it be celebration or grief, we have won because we have Him! We have found something greater than gold and given up our "toys," as Tozer prayed.

Psalm 139:11–12 states, "If I say, 'Surely the darkness shall cover me, and the light about me be night,' even the darkness is not dark to you; the night is bright as the day, for darkness is as light with you." Even the darkest parts of your story and mine, the most shame-filled of the "pity clap" moments we are constantly reminded of, are not dark because He makes them light. We were not made to know shame before Adam and Eve sinned in the garden of Eden, and when we are abiding in the goodness of God's presence, He helps to restore some forms of Eden in our hearts and minds.

3

Living in the Dark Night

W hen I started at Baylor, my mom and little brother flew out to Texas with me to move me in and get me settled. We went to all the meetings, met all the people, and did all the "freshmen things." I had been working through injuries all summer, so I wasn't in the best shape when I first got there, but I was working hard and slowly but surely starting to get back into good running shape. Things were looking up as the fall semester began.

Around halfway through the season, I was in good race shape again. I really felt like I was about to become the old me I had dreamed of so many times. That is, until I tore my second hip. When that happened, I was gradually sidelined over the course of the rest of the season as the pain got so bad I could not even function with high-dose pain meds. And as the pain and disappointment began to worsen, so did my negative habits around food and my body.

I think a lot of college freshmen struggle with negative habits or insecurities because it is their first time away from home and everything feels so new, and I was no different. One thing I struggled with when I got there was thinking I wasn't skinny enough. If you're a runner, or maybe just a female in general, you know what I am talking about. The pressure to look super skinny in a sports bra and spandex all the time ate at me more than I would like to admit. Terms like "race weight," "fit," and "tiny" were thrown around so much. Although honestly, any insecurities around food or my body had started during the first few injuries in high school when I felt like I needed something in my life I could control. I was never clinically diagnosed with an eating disorder or depression, but this first season in college was definitely the closest I'd ever been.

I was in a constant cycle of restricting and binging food. Being so alone and missing my family led to nights full of bingeing on foods I did not even want to consume. If you have ever struggled with bulimia or bingeing, you know it is hard to explain or open up to people about it. I have only recently started sharing about my experience openly. I kept it a secret because I was embarrassed and ashamed of myself. It's funny how good the enemy is at convincing us everyone will quit loving us or think we are weird if they know the truth about what we struggle with.

In what areas has the enemy tried to steal your confidence and joy? I do not think we all struggle with the same forms of insecurities, but I do know we all struggle. It is hard when something looks completely different from what we had dreamed. What is an area in your life where you feel like a dream got broken? Where you just wanted to yell, "God, it's not supposed to be this way! What did I do wrong?"

I remember one morning when the team was not having

practice, and I had signed up to use the anti-gravity treadmill for my long run because I was still in too much pain to run on the ground. I had been upset and binged the night before and felt I needed to purge by getting this run in to burn off the calories.

I got up at 5 a.m. and made my way to the track training room. No one else was there since it was not training room hours. My hip was hurting so badly by the end of mile one, even with the treadmill gravity percentage very low, so I had to stop. My planned ten-mile "purge" for the night before was sabotaged. Instead of the big calorie burn I "needed" to feel better about myself, I could not even finish one mile.

I was so upset that I felt like I had to binge again to make myself feel better. So, I grabbed eight or ten sugary granola bars from the training room and ate them in my car while crying before going back to my dorm to get ready for class and pretend like everything was okay.

Another weekend, when my roommates were all gone, I binged so badly that I tried to make myself physically purge by throwing up. For some reason, no matter how hard I tried, my body just would not throw up. Now, I am so thankful the Lord did not allow me to create a bad habit in that form of purging. However, at the moment, I was so mad at myself for bingeing and furthering my shame and insecurity. I thought throwing up was the only answer, and I could not get myself to do it. I cried myself to sleep alone in that freshman dorm room most nights, but this night, I had a little bit more pain in my chest than the normal tear-filled nights.

Looking back on those nights, I still think, *Wow, that was hard!* But I also see and feel God hugging me during those times more than ever before. I have said this before, but I know this and believe it: God brings us to our lowest for His highest.

Writing these stories down brings me to tears all over again. I can only remember fractions of how hard those "dark nights" that turned into days that turned back into "dark nights" were. But those nights were when God taught me that no matter how sad or alone I felt, He would absolutely never leave me. I learned to lean on Him in new ways, one day at a time. It was painful, but I was learning.

I also cry thinking of them because I think of you, who may be in your own cycle of binge eating, depression, suicidal thoughts, anxiety attacks, or more. I cry for you. It is so easy to see the bitterness instead of the blessing in our stories, but I want you to see Him as your Helper so badly. I want you to know He doesn't waste anything, and He bottles up your tears (Ps. 56:8). It is painful, but you are learning too, so lean in.

I know these stories I've shared carry a lot of heavy pain and disappointment. If you are still in the midst of that heaviness with your own season, I want to dive into practical ways we can lean on the Lord.

HE COMES TO STEAL, KILL, AND DESTROY

I think the hardest part about knowing God is using "dark nights" and hard seasons is hearing His voice above the enemy's voice. The enemy comes to steal our hope, kill our joy, and destroy our light. I want to dive into how we can beat him at his game of darkness and lies. How do we do that? By knowing the truth and light. So, let's jump into the three areas where the enemy attacks us most.

1. He Steals Our Hope

I think the first thing we have to realize is who the enemy is—a liar. He sneaks in and steals our hope by slowly but surely convincing us, "It is always going to be this way." He tells us that whatever tough circumstances we are in are never going away, and it will only get worse from here. He wants us to feel sorry for ourselves and take no action to get out of the hard or bad situations we find ourselves in.

Change comes from action, and the enemy knows that. Regarding the enemy's strategy in reference to a person's motivation to act, C. S. Lewis states, "The more often he feels without acting, the less he will be able ever to act, and, in the long run, the less he will be able to feel."[1] Satan's goal is to make you bitter and make you forget the hope you have in Christ. Because if he can make you bitter, he can keep you from the blessing God has for you and the blessing you could be to others. So, he steals our hope by saying, "It is always going to be this way."

2. He Kills Our Joy

How does he kill our joy? Well, I am sure you have heard the saying, "Comparison is the thief of all joy." I believe, especially with the age of social media we live in, comparison is one of the hardest things to overcome. It can make us want to be mad at someone all the time simply because they are doing well.

I want to share a story of the first time I ever intensely struggled with comparison and how the enemy stole my joy. I want you to think of similar stories in your own life as you read it. What are some areas where you may be holding on to bitterness toward someone when they did nothing wrong? This could be stealing your joy, just like it did mine.

How many of us have dreamed of a cute house with our dream boy once we are married? We dream about that house, how we will decorate it, the memories we will make there, the meals we will cook, the guests we will have, the neighborhood we love, and walks to our favorite coffee shop. Our first three months of marriage were this dream home come true for Casey and me!

We lived on the BeltLine right near Ponce City Market in downtown Atlanta. We could walk to the gym, açai bowl shops, and coffee shops. Anywhere we wanted to go was steps from our dreamy loft-style apartment. Our morning routine looked like snuggling, reading, coffee, and walks to the gym. We loved living there. Our sublease was only for three months, though, and we had to move out.

Long story short, we were supposed to move to an apartment complex in the Atlanta neighborhood of Buckhead within the next month. We would get an amazing deal because I was helping start the coffee shop underneath the apartments, but construction kept getting pushed further and further back. So, we moved in with my parents to wait it out.

Three months into our marriage, and we were living with my parents. Do not get me wrong—I love my family so much. My parents are amazing and blessed us so much by letting us live with them. But I missed the city so much, and I missed my friends. We lived in the upstairs storage room with all of my siblings' old clothes and grandmother's knick-knacks. I was commuting over an hour to work at 4 a.m. to open the gym I worked at and working double shifts until 8 or 9 p.m. I was exhausted during this time and remember telling myself one day, "Calm down, Kathryn, it is just a season."

I remember driving to open the gym at 4 a.m. the first morning we lived with my parents. I stopped for gas in the cold on the way to Atlanta. After filling up my tank and trying to stay positive about how great work would be that day, I passed the exit we used to live off of ten minutes away from work, and I absolutely broke down in tears while driving. I felt sorry for myself that I did not live in the city anymore. Later that day, during my shift, my boss told me what a good job I was doing, and she wanted to give me a raise. I was super thankful, and it made the rough morning drive feel less bad!

Even in the midst of good things like being a newlywed, getting a raise, and having a roof over my head, I struggled with contentment in that season. I remember feeling so jealous of young married friends who had their own cute place in the city to make home. You may be like, *Why? You still had so much to be grateful for!* And to that, I would say: You are right, and later in this chapter I will talk about a gratitude check I had.

God convicted me throughout the next week. I truly am so blessed, but I had been wanting to feel sorry for myself. I think we do this a lot in life. We want to play the victim because it feels good. We want to make someone else look bad for what they have because we struggle with discontentment. I think this is right where the enemy wants us. Sometimes, the truth is hard to believe, but it sets us free from our self-obsession and gets our gaze back on Jesus instead of our circumstances!

So, (1) the enemy stole my hope because I was so focused on my current circumstances never getting better, and (2) he killed my joy over my boss giving me a raise by skewing my perspective of what others had and I did not. I let my jealousy of their circumstances get in the way of the celebration of those young married friends! How often do we do this as believers? We have so much worth celebrating, but the enemy is so good at what he does. He is a killer and a thief.

3. He Destroys Our Light

Let's move on to the final thing the enemy tries to do: destroy our light. This last one is a little different than the others because it is much harder for him to accomplish. The light we carry is Jesus, and the enemy cannot destroy Jesus or the good news we carry with us. However, he can cause us to doubt Jesus or walk away from the calling God has for us.

The enemy uses stealing and killing to get to this part—the destroying. Once he makes us weak, it is much easier to accomplish his ultimate goal. He does not want you to go to heaven and he surely does not want you to convince others to go with you.

I want to dive into what the Bible says about the light we carry. In 2 Corinthians 4:5–6, Paul states: "For what we proclaim is not ourselves, but Jesus Christ as Lord, with ourselves as your servants for Jesus' sake. For God, who said, 'Let light shine out of darkness,' has shone in our hearts to give the light of the knowledge of the glory of God in the face of Jesus Christ." So, we know that Jesus is this "light" in our hearts, and the devil is the darkness of the world. The darkness will always try to beat the light, even though Jesus already won through the cross and resurrection.

Our call as believers—the thing that brings us the most hope and joy—is coming alongside Jesus and being a light to this dark world. I believe one of the major reasons I struggled as intensely as I did in college was because I was not focused on what God could do *through* me but on what God could do *for* me.

Many of us dream of being successful, beautiful, and popular. I was doing some research on statistics of what our generation aspires to be and found these statements regarding the personal values and life outlook of Gen Z:

1. "Making money and having a successful career are the two most universally important life goals for Gen Z adults—more than pursuing friends, family, or hobbies.

Seventy percent of Gen Z adults say making money is very important to them."

2. "Gen Z adults are more likely to define themselves by what they do, rather than who they are: Career choice and hobbies are the two most important concepts to shaping their personal identity, notably more than ideas like race or religion."

3. "Nearly a quarter of Gen Z adults have aspirations to be famous: 23% say being famous is important to them—eight points higher than millennials and 15 points higher than Gen X."[2]

These statements are wild if you actually sit back and take the time to read over them again. How has fame or money become more important than our faith or family? It seems to continue to flip more and more every generation. If we are not trained to dream differently than the world, then we will continue to be disappointed whether our dreams come true or get broken.

Because, let's be honest, even the most successful people who accomplished far more than they could have ever imagined almost always end up depressed and feeling like they are not enough. As I was doing some of this research, I came across a *People* magazine article titled, "Celeb Confessions That'll Make You Never Want to Be Famous." Some of the celebrity confessions they listed were as follows:

- Amanda Seyfried: Anxiety & Panic Attacks Caused by Fame Feels Like "Life or Death"
- Daniel Radcliffe: It's Tempting to Turn to Alcohol to Cope with Scrutiny

- Billie Eilish: You're Basically Miserable Half of the Time
- Gigi Hadid: You Lose a Lot of Friends
- Idris Elba: Fame Makes You Paranoid
- George Clooney: You Can't Enjoy Simple Pleasures
- Selena Gomez: There's Nothing but Constant Pressure
- Justin Bieber: People Kick You When You're Down
- Lady Gaga: You "Belong to Everyone Else"[3]

I don't exactly need to prove my point here, these celebrities' statements do it for me. The world and hustle culture will never fulfill us. Only Jesus, the Light of the world, can do that. So, the only true fulfilling thing in this life is the thing Satan tries to keep us from. He will distract us with every other item in the playbook to keep us away from what God has for us.

However, if we can turn off the distractions and tune in to what God is doing in our lives, we will begin to see why the enemy works so hard to keep us from being light to the world. We will realize how fulfilling this kingdom work is.

EVEN THE DARKNESS IS NOT DARK TO YOU

After graduating college and marrying Casey, I have come back to thinking about those hard, tear-filled nights at Baylor many times. I am so thankful I am fulfilled in what God is doing in my life now. It is even sweeter to know what He walked me through before and where I am today because it gives me more confidence to continue to walk in His way when things get hard. When I get tempted to be distracted because, trust me, I do, I can remind myself of all He has walked me through and that He will continue to be with me.

I want to leave you with one more thing before we end this chapter and move on to how hope can begin to heal us from disappointment. I want you to know if you are still walking through your "dark night," it is not all dark. Jesus is holding you closer than you know. You will be able to look back someday and see that He was bottling up your tears and did not waste any of it. I pray you learn to know and trust Him in this valley like you never have before.

I also pray you work hard to find a community to share your burdens with. The enemy wants you to go it alone and keep your most shame-filled secrets to yourself because it is far easier for him to lie to you that way. But I promise you, when all you want to do is run and hide, it is so worth it to put in the work to go on a coffee date or join a Bible study. It will change your life.

Decide today—maybe even write a promise to yourself and God in your journal—that you will give your lowest for God's highest. Commit to not wasting your pain and to leaning into what God is calling you to. Decide to live out being the light of the world because once you step into this action of shining Christ's light as your primary joy and purpose, any chance the enemy had at destroying your light fades into the darkness.

As I shared in the previous chapter, Psalm 139:12 says, "Even the darkness is not dark to you; the night is bright as the day, for darkness is as light with you." When you know the one who is the light, the dark is still hard and the grief is still real and heavy, but it is not endless because there is still hope and a light at the end of the tunnel in Christ.

4

Learning How to Heal

If you have never heard of Jay and Katherine Wolf or their book *Hope Heals*, add that to your reading list this year.[1] They are seriously some of the strongest people I have ever met. They met at Samford University, the school I graduated from. Jay fell for Katherine when he saw her in the cafeteria, and they continued to pursue their friendship together after that first meeting. Eventually, they got married and moved to California for Jay to finish law school at Pepperdine. So, why am I telling you about this random couple?

Well, Jay and Katherine have had a super big impact on my life and how I process things that happen to me. I was at a Passion Conference where Jay and Katherine spoke. It was my senior year in high school, and I had been really broken about my injuries. It was during the peak of when I was trying to decide where to go to college to run but not getting many scholarships because of the past two years of bad races since I had not been healthy.

After Passion was over, everyone asked what the best message or band was. Every time someone asked me, I said that Katherine was my favorite. I remember one of my friends said, "Why? That one made me a little sad." I said it was because I related so heavily to Katherine. Katherine had a stroke and almost died after they moved to California. Her journey has been incredibly hard, but she and Jay have made the Lord their hope and purpose beyond the pain. Katherine missed her old life but decided to choose hope over despair and help a lot of people along the way. I related to her story not because I had experienced a stroke or disability but because I was in a dark place with my injuries.

I missed winning races and how running made me feel, and I could not do those things, so my future felt hopeless. Even if, to the world, my "handicap" was nowhere near as severe as Katherine's, it still felt crippling to me. I was so thankful to see someone like Katherine able to stand up against her pain with Jesus as her helper because it made me believe I could get through what I was going through too.

One of my favorite things I remember hearing Katherine say often, whether in her writing or on a stage speaking, is "everyone's heart is in some kind of wheelchair."[2] Sure, I do not have a physical wheelchair, and you might not, either. But we all have unseen hurts we get to fight through. The enemy wants us to despair, but Christ is waiting for us to realize the glorious hope He offers. Back then, I was allowing my current disappointment with life to cripple me more than Katherine's physical wheelchair. I was letting the hurt hold me back, while Katherine was looking "further up and further in,"[3] knowing Christ was her only true hope. She had allowed a hope greater than the world's idea of success to heal her and was not letting the hurt stop her. She was in a wheelchair, but man, was she doing damage for the kingdom!

When she shared at Passion, I cried because I felt like she was with me in my pain. Then, she inspired me with a perspective of purpose in pain—pain as a platform, not a handicap. God does not waste anything, particularly not pain.

FURTHER UP, FURTHER IN

Shortly after Casey and I started dating, my family and I left for a week to serve at Hope Heals Camp, Jay and Katherine's camp for families looking for hope in the middle of disability. My sister and I had come to camp as "compassionate companions" (what they call the volunteers there) for the past two years, and now our whole family was coming. It was such a special week for all of us to be together in-the-middle-of-nowhere Alabama to serve and learn from the Wolfs and everyone there.

Being around people who love, serve, and preach so hard like Jay and Katherine grows you more than most things can. Worshiping early in the morning in our little cabin Bible study with all of the volunteers was so special. Standing beside my dad and little brother at 7 a.m. was such a sweet experience. Seeing my dad serve at Hope Heals was so cool because I knew it was out of his comfort zone to get out of his routine, stay at a campsite with young kids, eat camp food, take vacation time off work, and serve. I knew serving at camp humbled him, and he was okay with being humbled for the sake of the gospel.

We all need to be okay with being humbled a little more. If it brings me closer to the feet of Jesus, I want it. I want to be more like my dad and more like Jay and Katherine. I want to live my life full of humility, knowing the source of hope that heals and wanting to bring that healing to others.

Whenever I bring up something I am struggling with to my mom, she always asks me, "Well, where are you serving?" She listens to my problems and has empathy for me, but she also reminds me that getting my focus off myself and onto others and how I can serve them helps to heal me!

You might be thinking, *Wait, isn't serving others what Martha did in the Bible when Jesus told her to rest and be more like Mary?* I first mentioned Mary and Martha in chapter 1 as the sisters of Lazarus. But that's not the only place we read about them in Scripture. In Luke 10, there is a story about Jesus eating dinner at their house. During dinner, Mary is simply sitting at Jesus' feet, so attentive and excited to hear the stories He has to tell. Mary has left Martha to do all the hosting and serving for Jesus and His disciples. Martha asks Jesus to tell Mary to help her, and He says, "You are worried and upset about many things, but few things are needed—or indeed only one. Mary has chosen what is better, and it will not be taken away from her" (Luke 10:41–42 NIV).

Sometimes, we are simply serving because we think we *have* to, and we are checking something off the list like Martha was in the Bible. While sitting and resting at the feet of Jesus is always necessary, taking our eyes off ourselves can help us fix our eyes on Him. A verse I shared at a retreat for girls who struggle with body image talks about how, ironically, we can actually make ourselves idols and glory in our own shame if we are not careful. Philippians 3:17–21 says:

> Brothers, join in imitating me, and keep your eyes on
> those who walk according to the example you have in us.
> For many, of whom I have often told you and now tell you
> even with tears, walk as enemies of the cross of Christ.
> Their end is destruction, their god is their belly, and they
> glory in their shame, with minds set on earthly things. But
> our citizenship is in heaven, and from it we await a Savior,
> the Lord Jesus Christ, who will transform our lowly body

to be like his glorious body, by the power that enables him even to subject all things to himself.

We have to keep our eyes on what lies ahead. We have to keep our eyes on heaven and off our own "self" confidence. We need to be dialed in on storing up treasure in heaven, not running after treasures on this earth that do not even last or fulfill. True fulfillment and joy come from this "further up and further in"[4] perspective.

BUT I WANTED IT MY WAY . . .

Another one-liner by Katherine Wolf I love is: "I get to fix my eyes on the grace gift of existing, rather than the shame of imperfections."[5] We live in a beauty-obsessed culture. The global beauty industry is worth $511 billion.[6] They want us to feel more insecure because they make more money when we think we need another quick beauty fix. Even if you get more fit or fix the thing in your life that is going wrong, there will always be another thing that can bring us shame and sadness if we decide to dwell on it. We have to learn how to surrender the hard things—the struggle—to God and ask Him for the help to keep our gaze locked on heaven and what He has for us.

When I went through a really bad breakup in college, I was brokenhearted afterward. I thought I would never get over it. The number one thing that helped me heal during all that was serving and being involved in my local college ministry with my church. I also stepped down from running in college around that same time and was able to serve on mission trips and kids camps. These brought so much fulfillment and healing.

If I had not poured into others during those hard times, I

believe the healing would have been ten times more difficult because it would have been "all about me" and what I had "lost" because my life looked different now. Instead, while that season was still hard, it was filled with absolute awe and wonder at the doors God was opening for jobs, school, friendship, community, and so many other amazing things. I was able to see where He was blessing me because I was not bitter about what was going on in my life.

I think so often we get in a "poor me" mindset like Paul talks about in Philippians 3:18–19, and it keeps us from the blessing God has—the hope that is in the healing.

You will be so blessed by God's character in hard times if you lean in and ask Him to teach you something through the pain. Our God does not waste pain and is on the edge of His seat, waiting to walk you through this and bottle up your tears along the way. I want you to take a moment to reflect on the few verses from Acts 20, where Paul is talking about his life and ministry:

> "And now, behold, I am going to Jerusalem, constrained by the Spirit, not knowing what will happen to me there, except that the Holy Spirit testifies to me in every city that imprisonment and afflictions await me. But I do not account my life of any value nor as precious to myself, if only I may finish my course and the ministry that I received from the Lord Jesus, to testify to the gospel of the grace of God. . . . For I did not shrink from declaring to you the whole counsel of God. . . . And now I commend you to God and to the word of his grace, which is able to build you up and to give you the inheritance among all those who are sanctified. I coveted no one's silver or gold or

apparel. You yourselves know that these hands ministered to my necessities and to those who were with me. In all things I have shown you that by working hard in this way we must help the weak and remember the words of the Lord Jesus, how he himself said, 'It is more blessed to give than to receive.'" (Acts 20:22–24, 27, 32–35)

Now, I think we can all agree we like to get *our* way. We like things to go just as we plan the first time we try them. However, once things have finally gone wrong enough times and we decide to surrender them to God, we often end up realizing how much better God's way was all along. It is not better because it is easier or better in the world's eyes, but because when we do it God's way, we get to experience dependence and intimacy with a faithful Father and friend. So, we learn to realize that even though, no, it does not come naturally, it truly is more blessed to give than to receive, as Paul reminds us. When we experience the hope and generosity of a good Father in our lives, we want to be more like Him.

EMET

I was recently studying what it means to "have faith" or to "be faithful" in the long run as a believer. I always hear the word *faith* discussed in a hard way, when someone is believing or praying for something specific, they are to "have faith" for it. But what does it mean as believers to be faithful, not just have faith *for* something?

The Bible was originally written in Hebrew and Greek, so I looked up what the word *faithful* was in Hebrew. It is *emet*, which means "the truth."[7] However, as we look at Scripture in more detail, we find many other references to this word *emet*. There are several places where the word *emet* is used to offer different contextual meanings than just "the truth." Exodus 17:12 uses the term to mean the physical stability or reliability of an object when Moses is holding his staff over a battle between Amalek and the Israelites, and he needs the strength to keep his staff *emet*, or steady.[8] Then, in Exodus 18:21, the word is used in reference to someone with a trustworthy character when Moses' father-in-law is telling him what kind of leaders he needs to appoint to help him guide the Israelites.[9] Therefore, the fact that God is faithful, or *emet*, does not only mean that He is the truth or stands for the truth, but that He is a steady and trustworthy friend.

When we learn more about how faithful our God is to us, we are encouraged to be more faithful to Him. God is not faithful because He makes life easy for us or does everything we want Him to do, but because it is His character. We all know the Scripture where it talks about how we want to hear, "Well done, good and faithful servant" (Matt. 25:23), when we get to heaven. How then do we as believers be faithful? How do we remember every day that we serve a God who deserves us being willing to be on mission, serving His people for His honor and His glory? This is the hope that heals.

The only thing truly trustworthy, good, and fulfilling in this world is our Jesus! We have to realize the self-gratifying ways of the world will not satisfy us when being faithful to our Jesus is the only way to be truly hopeful or fulfilled. When you look up the Hebrew word for *trust*, it is the word *he'emin*, meaning to trust or to have trust.[10] But underneath the meaning of this word when you look it up in a dictionary or google it, you will see the explanation that it is the *verb* form of the word *emet*.

Therefore, that means trusting is the verb form of faithfulness.[11]

So, these lifelong questions of "How do we feel fulfilled?" and "How can we be more faithful?" are easily answered with "Simply trust." We cannot go wrong or be unfaithful when we are trusting God and acting on that because it is, in fact, the verb or action form of being faithful.

Deciding where to go to college was a trying process for me. I had been dealing with injuries and health issues for over two years by that point. College coaches did not see a nationally ranked runner anymore. They saw "injured," "has been," "red flag," and "just another girl trying to get a walk-on spot." I was struggling with identity, depression, and some forms of disordered eating. Overall, I was not in a good or very happy time in my life. I was struggling to be faithful and trust that God was working good in my life in the midst of all these broken dreams when it came to running.

I remember when my mom and I were flying to Baylor for my official visit there. I played worship music as I boarded the plane. I was listening to Lauren Daigle, and one of her songs I had never heard before came on. It was called "Trust in You." In it, she talks about surrendering our dreams to Jesus, even when He does not give an answer as to *why* we are having to go through whatever we are facing.

As I've already mentioned, I loved Lauren's music during this time period of my life. The lyrics to her songs had such a desperate cry of surrendering it all and trusting God. I wondered what Lauren's story was to be able to develop such a deep cry in her music. It turns out that in her teen years, Daigle was unable to go to school or perform in public spaces because she had cytomegalovirus, which weakened her immune system to where even common illnesses could cause a major threat to her. Since her immune system was so weak, she had to spend two years almost entirely alone.[12]

Her mother did not want her to be depressed, so she signed Lauren up for voice lessons, and she fell in love with it. She says it became her healing, and her songs spring from the wealth God allowed her to experience in those two overwhelming years.[13] God used her "dark night" moments, alone and on her knees on the bedroom floor, to build her faith, to activate her trust muscle, and to help her walk into what He was calling her to do. Then, He healed her.

When Daigle was in the "dark night," it would have seemed impossible that she would lead worship from a stage someday if she could not even leave her house because of this sickness. What God was calling her to did not seem to make sense in her current circumstances. But the place that she thought would overwhelm her because it was so hard became the launching point God used to develop that deep cry in her lyrics. Her songs impact hundreds of millions of people all over the globe and help people experience the presence of the hope that heals.

I want to encourage you with Lauren's story. If you keep fixing your eyes on Jesus, if you can keep activating that trust muscle and saying, "God, You are my biggest dream," then when it seems like every other dream has broken, He will use that as your launching pad. He will use that to grow your faith so you can do more to bring honor and glory to His name. The reason I have such a desire to speak to high school and college-aged women is because of the burden I remember bearing and because I saw what healing hope was brought into my life when I decided to fully believe my God was *emet*, or faithful.

GIVING BACK

When I won the *USA Today* National Guard Inspiration Award in high school in 2014, my mom told me years later that she had asked God, "What did she do to win this award?" She heard God say, "She will need this for later." In the article *USA Today* did, I stated this regarding a mission trip I had just gone on:

> Giving back changes your perspective and your attitude about what you have. If you just go to a movie with a friend, you'll remember the movie, and it'll be a fun time, but the people you impact by volunteering will always remember. That's way more important. . . . Many people have poured into my life. I just want to give back at least a little bit of what people have poured into me.[14]

I recognized at such an early age the importance of this "giving back," as Paul talks about in Acts. I actually ended up receiving that award in a boot. I had a bad fall the week before the ceremony and hurt my foot and tore my hip muscle. It was the major injury that started the ripple effect of injuries for eight years to follow.

I thought injuries would break me many times throughout my journey. I actually still cry about my injuries multiple times a week because they still hurt and it is still hard. I walked home from a two-mile run just yesterday, crying and asking God for "the why." The hip pain from that fall when I tore my right labral never got better and still makes me limp home from *most* of the runs I do today because it is chronic.

Jesus does not promise us a pain-free life. We are not in the perfect garden of Eden anymore, and we most definitely are not in heaven yet. Therefore, life will not always feel good, and it will be hard to be faithful because we are not home yet. But while we are still exiles on this earth, we get to consciously decide to wake up every single day and pray, "Lord, I know fixing my eyes on You, the Author and Perfecter of my faith, is the only way to be fulfilled. Please fill me with Your hope that heals when the pain is still there. Please show me the area You would have me serve in to show more people your hope that can heal them too. Amen."

We are all walking each other home in different ways as we wade through life's joy and chaos together. I hope we can all be a little more like Katherine Wolf and Lauren Daigle and make good out of the bad that life hands us as we serve one another along the way. If we can learn to still have hope in the midst of our healing, we can, in turn, help so many others around us to heal as well.

5

When You Don't Want the Story God Is Writing

We have talked a lot about painful seasons, hard seasons, and "dark night" seasons. Why? Because we all walk through them; it is relatable. And because I want you to see the importance of making Jesus number one, even in the hard times, before you make it out to the other side.

C. S. Lewis wrote a book called *The Problem of Pain.*[1] I love that title because pain is just that—a problem. When we come to know God as a good Father, it is hard to explain or make sense of the troubles that we face in life. I believe we overcome this confusion simply by allowing it to be what it is—confusing. We very often, in fact, *do not* get the why, when, and how from God. However, we do always know that God is good and we are here to do His will.

Sometimes, we do not want the story God is writing. But guess what? He is the Author. I am truly sorry if you do not like how I wrote something in this book, but it cannot be changed now. The author has written it, and it is in print. I can promise you that even when your pain is problematic, God the Author did not make a misprint. He does not "make" bad things happen to us in life, but I believe what He allows, He uses. My dad once told me, "What He calls for, He pays for." And friend, He will use your story.

I remember one of the first times it really hit me that God wanted to use me, my story, my life—whatever you want to call it. I was going through a really hard breakup and praying about quitting running. I was finishing my last few races of the season with my team before making my final decision, though. The first race back after the breakup, I remember racing very badly and feeling horrible because I had been too sad and drained to sleep or eat much that week. I was heartbroken and struggling. Trying to run an all-out 6k race against D1 athletes was not exactly easy at the time with everything going on.

After the race, I was cooling down on the track by myself, and my mom came over to talk with me because she knew I was upset. I started crying about how bummed I was. In the middle of the conversation, another mom from a different team whose daughter had run that day came up to us and told me that her daughter followed me on Instagram. She said her daughter always talked about my posts about my injuries with encouraging captions. She told me how much they had helped her daughter when she was at the end of her rope. She talked for a few minutes, was super kind, and ended the conversation by saying, "Don't you ever stop."

As soon as she left, I started bawling to my mom again. I said, "See, I know I am helping people. I know God is using it all. But Mom . . . it is so hard. Mom, I just want to be fast again so bad. I am so tired of hurting all the time. I know He is using it, but it is so hard."

I often think back to this conversation when I am discouraged or feel I am not doing enough. When things get hard in life, it is okay to acknowledge it and say, "Yes, this is hard." But we have to remember to pause in the middle of the problematic pain and say, "I won't ever stop because I know God is using me."

I shared online some about the miscarriages Casey and I walked through during our fertility journey in our marriage. I wanted to help other women and couples going through fertility struggles to feel less alone. I had people say wildly hurtful things to me about how "I should keep that kind of thing to myself" or that I was "wildly dramatic and miscarriage and fertility is not something 'hard' I am overcoming." I agree that being overly vulnerable online if you are not ready or it is not the time or place can be damaging and misplaced. But I knew I was sharing exactly what God wanted me to at that time. I received hundreds of messages a day from women all over the world walking through the lonely and hopeless feeling of grief that comes with fertility struggles and miscarriages. They would say how much my videos or captions had helped them keep going and keep hoping.

In life, there will be times when "our story" is not for everyone, but God uses it for someone. People who have not walked through the same thing as you cannot possibly understand it. But a hardship you might be walking through is developing empathy, compassion, and a listening ear for someone who might never have someone else who understands, and that is the gift of your story, whether it is for one or one million.

PRETTY FEET

We have to be so firm and confident in the purpose of being a light that nothing and no one can ever convince us it is not worth trying or fighting for. My dad's and my favorite verse growing up was Isaiah 52:7. It says, "How beautiful upon the mountains are the feet of him who brings good news . . . who says to Zion, 'Your God reigns.'" I loved that verse growing up simply because my daddy read it to me every morning.

We love coffee in my family, and even when I was five or six, my dad was making me a cup of coffee (mostly cream and sugar) every morning. It had become a bit of a tradition for him to make me my small, sugary "coffee" every morning while he read to me. We were homeschooled until late middle to high school, so we got to start our mornings out a little slower than some, and my dad started every morning with his Bible.

I remember those mornings with him so fondly because I learned so much about Jesus and heard so many Bible stories that my dad would explain to me. Every time, without fail, we would end the session by reading Isaiah 52:7. It was our verse. My dad nicknamed me "pretty feet" from the verse since it talks about a messenger having "beautiful feet." All throughout high school and college, I had different life verses when people asked, and sometimes, I would say this one because it was special to me. Just within the past two to three years post-college, God has really revealed more of the meaning of this special verse to me. The Lord has given it a new meaning in my life.

A little over a year ago, I started planning a retreat called "Be a Blessing" for girls who struggle with disordered eating and insecurities. As I was planning, I kept asking God what the theme verse should be. He kept telling me it was Isaiah 52:7. I was hesitant because this verse does not inherently have anything to do with body image.

However, as I continued to plan the retreat and pray over the themes, I heard a sermon on the context of this Scripture. They discussed how, at that time, if a battle or war broke out between two cities, they would always send a messenger with a scroll to the battlefield. That messenger's sole job was to run back to the town or city after the battle, with the scroll saying whether they lost or won. His job was pretty important because he was coming back to the wives and children of the soldiers to tell them if their husbands and brothers were coming home alive from war. He was bringing the news of whether or not their town was about to be enslaved by their enemy. His scroll was pretty important. In that day, they wore sandals or no shoes at all, so we can be sure that this verse is not literally talking about his *feet* being beautiful after running through the mountains. The reason his feet were so beautiful to this town was because, in the context of this Scripture, they *won* the battle. In Isaiah 52, the messenger is returning with good news of a battle won, declaring victory and a homecoming.

So, what is the reason for this soul being called beautiful? I can promise you it had nothing to do with his dirty, grimy feet that just ran across the mountains. It had everything to do with the message he was carrying. What if that is true of us as well? When we feel insecure about our outward beauty or our purpose (inward beauty), what if we get to have confidence in something else? In the midst of pain, in the midst of heartbreak, in the midst of insecurity or shame, we get to say, "My confidence does not lie here." We get to rest in the knowledge that the good news of victory we carry—the light of the world inside us—is the most beautiful thing about us.

Many of us know the phrase "going from a victim to a victor." When we know what Jesus did for us and believe in that— when we accept Him into our hearts and lives—He becomes the good news we carry and the most beautiful thing about us. The problem of pain still exists, but there is a reminder inside and all around us that says, "There is still good news. The ulti-mate good news is that we have already won."

REFRACTIONS ARE CATCHING

Once we know this, what changes, though? Once we realize sharing this good news is actually the most fulfilling thing we can walk out, where do we go from there?

We transform our mind so we can live it out. We make it head *and* heart knowledge, a part of our identity and purpose, and not just something we think about when we are feeling good. One of the most revolutionary books I have ever read, which came in and challenged a lot of what I thought walking out my faith as a believer looked like, was *Renovation of the Heart* by Dallas Willard. On transforming the mind, he states:

> The person and gospel of Jesus Christ—building on simple "Jesus loves me, this I know, for the Bible tells me so"—is the only complete answer to the false and destructive images and ideas that control the life of those away from God. The process of spiritual formation in Christ is one of progressively replacing those destructive images and ideas with the images and ideas that filled the mind of Jesus himself. We thereby come increasingly to see "the light of the gospel of the glory of Christ, who is the image of God" (2 Corinthians 4:4 NRSV).[2]

In general, it is hard to rule our minds and say no to negative thoughts that come up—to know that God's thoughts are higher than our thoughts and His ways are better than ours. Sometimes, we do not want the story God is writing because "His ways are not our ways" (Isa. 55:8–9), and we like to get things *our* way. In Matthew 16:23, Jesus calls Peter, one of His disciples, "Satan" or the "Adversary" because Peter was thinking in human, sinful terms. God called him out to separate how radically different God's ideas and images are than ours. We can only escape conforming to a fallen humanity by putting on the mind of Christ Himself.

Now, as believers, it is pretty important for us to "get" this message. For us to understand how to transform our mind because, as Dallas Willard writes, "The prosperity of God's cause on earth depends upon his people thinking well."[3]

I like to think of it this way: When you put a disco ball in a dark room and shine one tiny light on it, it sends refractions of light all over. You, shining in the middle of your "dark night," shed the light and glory and hope of Jesus on a friend. Then that friend gets coffee with three of their friends, who go home and encourage their siblings, who then go back to their college campuses and start a Bible study, and that Bible study has a future communicator in it, who then goes all over the world years later proclaiming the gospel of Jesus from a stage.

We are not all called to be on a stage or be speakers. But we *are* all called to light up a dark world and send refractions of God's glory all over. Because the thing about refractions is, they are catching. The shine from one disco ball can shine onto a different disco ball in the same dark room, and it sends more glimmers of light all over. There are a lot of figurative "disco balls" in our dark world. They just need a little light shined on them before they can refract something beautiful once they catch the light. There are a whole lot of people who need reminding that the most beautiful thing about them is proclaiming the goodness of what Jesus already did for them.

When that mom told me to "never stop" sharing the story

God was writing in my heart around the hard things I was going through, she was a light encouraging me in my dark place. And I went on to be a light to many friends on my campus and girls online afterward, who are now a light to those around them. That light helps ignite a spark in me, and my spark keeps going to fan other's flames. It is all right for us to feel the hard, to recognize once again that the pain of this life is a *problem*. But, as Frank Laubach says, "The simple program of Christ for winning the whole world is to make each person He touches magnetic enough with love to draw others."[4] It is, as they say, "Okay to not be okay," but at the end of the day, we need to come back to our Purpose Giver to help us get through whatever it is we are going through. If we keep our eyes fixed on our hard circumstances instead of on Him, then we stay stuck there for a lot longer. We are all broken and cannot be perfect, but we do have the capacity to keep doing our best to light up the world with love. To keep being a magnet for Christ to bring others into the beauty of living and abiding in our purpose in Jesus.

You might be reading this thinking, *All right, Kathryn, that is great and all. I do want to love like that, but I feel so unloved and broken.* You might be thinking, *How do I get to where I can love others well when I always feel this way?* Just like we talked about in chapter 3, the enemy is trying hard to eat away at your joy and hope. To convince you that it is always going to be this way. In the coming chapters, we are going to discuss heavily our identity beyond our feelings.

"WHO TOLD YOU?"

Before we address the practical ways in which we "switch on" our brains to help us overcome those feelings, I want to talk about how we can have the strength in the hard times to even make that decision to "try." One of my favorites, Bob Goff, on breaking free of our feelings, asks us:

> Do you need the courage to admit, even now, that you have been pretending to be something you are not? Are you a prisoner needing space to get real? Have you been distracted by your need to never seem weak or afraid or vulnerable? Are you spending weird amounts of time trying to control the people around you because your life on the inside is out of control? How much energy is that taking out of you—energy you could pour into something bigger and more beautiful than your insecurities?
>
> We're all inwardly insecure to some degree. What shrouds this from view is that each of us deals with our insecurities differently and, as a result, only some of us look outwardly insecure. Some people can speak in public while others can't. Some people are afraid of spiders, and others collect tarantulas. Some people get quiet as a church mouse when they are insecure, and others get mean as a rattlesnake. If you want to dazzle God, don't ignore, dismiss, or deny your insecurities, and don't overlook other people's odd behaviors as the groans of insecurities make their way to the surface. Understand and embrace these things instead. Don't let them take you prisoner. Figure out where they came from and send them back there. Master these feelings when they're blocking your way forward, and choose to live undistracted by them. We are not the average of the five most insecure people who have opinions about us; we're the product of the several most focused and undistracted people we successfully imitate.[5]

I love this perspective because he calls out the fact that, as humans, we all struggle with different levels of hard things, negative feelings, and insecurities. We *all* feel this "problem of pain" to some degree and sense that something is not as it should be in our lives. Bob Goff is reminding us that these feelings are not to be ignored but to be embraced and studied so we can beat them!

He says to figure out where they came from and send them back there. The "send them back there" we will discuss in more detail soon, but for now, I want to focus on the "figure out where they came from" piece. I have mentioned before that I have a heart for girls who struggle with disordered eating and body image issues. One of the top things girls ask me is, "What do you do if you are having a bad body image day?" My answer is always to think about who told you the thoughts that are determining your feelings.

I remember one year when I was at Passion Conference with some of my high school friends. Christine Caine spoke on how to call out shame-filled thoughts as lies. She spoke on how knowing who is saying something determines its validity.[6] For example, if I am having bad thoughts about my body being ugly or that I am not good enough or that people hate me, I can simply ask the question, "Who told you that?" In research, people have to find valid sources because if a source is unreliable, the information it carries may not be factual. It is the same with emotions! Sometimes, feelings are not facts, and we need to assess who or what made us feel bad about ourselves and how we can overcome that feeling.

During a certain season in college, I used this question quite often. I was going through a bad breakup, had just quit running, and was really struggling with purpose in my life. My body had started to change because I was no longer doing a collegiate sport, and I was working three jobs and serving at church every other day. So, I was often too busy to have time to work out or too broke to buy certain foods. I remember the thoughts that were swirling around in my head.

When these bad thought life days occurred, I would plan to get up a little extra early the next day. My 5 a.m. alarm would go off in my tiny dorm room filled with graphics of encouraging quotes my nonartistic self had done my best to paint. I would turn on the lights I had strung all around the room and get out the tiny fifteen-dollar coffee pot my parents bought me for Christmas at the beginning of school, then play worship music while a yummy pot of hot coffee brewed. I would make my bed and get my favorite journal and pen out. And, right as the sun was beginning to come up on campus, I'd sip on my coffee and write down on the left side of a notebook page every insecure thought or doubt I was having. On the right side, at the top of the page, I'd write "What God Says," and in the middle, I would write "Who Told You." After each insecurity was written down, I would assess whether it aligned with what God's Word said and whether the person who told me that thing was valid. I would determine its *value*.

Honestly, most times, no one told me the thoughts I had. They had just popped into my head, which means they were probably from the enemy and made to discourage me. After seeing how invalid the person's opinion in the middle was, I would find the truth in God's Word of what was factual about me. Once I did the fact-checking of the source and found the insecurity faulty, I wouldn't leave it at that. I would go a step further to find Scripture to affirm the opposite of that thought and remind me of the truth. The truth really does set us free.

When girls ask me about what to do to help with these bad body image days, I always tell them to try this exercise. I know it can come off as cliché or like homework, but it works! Eventually, I quit writing it down and learned to simply assess each thought's validity as it came into my mind. And yes, I still have struggles, but I am much better about "tak[ing] every thought captive," as 2 Corinthians 10:5 says to do. Once we realize we feel a certain way because of our thought life, we can beat the enemy at his own game. All it takes is recognizing that a thought comes from the devil for us to realize it is invalid and ask God for help to dismiss it.

STOP, DROP, AND ROLL

In Hebrews 12:2, Paul tells us to fix our eyes on Jesus, who, "for the joy that was set before him endured the cross, despising its shame, and is seated at the right hand at the throne of God." Jesus went through the hardest of all hardship and took on the problem of all of our pain when He died on the cross for us. When we begin to glory in His sacrifice over our shame or self pity, we begin to form an identity in Christ that cannot be shaken by our feelings—and that is a powerful testimony.

C. S. Lewis reminds us throughout *The Problem of Pain* that we have to know our identity beyond our feelings. We have to know that no matter what emotions may come from our circumstances and thought life, our identity has to be firm enough to get us through these feelings and through the pain. We have to be so rooted in our identity as God's kids, as the light of the world, that nothing life throws at us and no amount of emotions can get us off course.

So when you have moments where it feels like you might get off course because the story God is writing is not what you dreamed, planned, and worked for, what are you going to do about it? Abide in Christ and in who He says you are. When you abide, you put out the fire of your anxious thoughts and feelings by stopping, dropping, and rolling. You stop what you are doing, drop to your knees, and listen to God's voice to help you roll out of whatever spiral you might have gotten into.

Life will always include disappointment. But when you learn to abide by getting familiar with your knees in God's presence, it is a bit easier to trust the Storyteller instead of continuing with the fiery anxiety and disappointment that can come when things do not go your way.

6

Your Identity Beyond Your Feelings

One summer, I was working at a running camp as a counselor. I had grown up going to this camp in the North Carolina mountains for a good portion of July every year. I would run sixty to seventy miles a week and hang out with some of my best friends at what was to us "the best week of summer!" But the summer I was a counselor, things were a little less dreamy than they had been in my camper years.

I was the fastest girl at the camp when I was attending in high school. Everyone liked me and wanted to be my friend because I was so successful, and it definitely boosted my confidence. However, a few years later, as a counselor, I was not as fast and had gained some weight because I had just gotten over another injury. I was dealing with disordered eating in the form of a binge-eating disorder. I had also gotten sunburned the week before, so my back, chest, and arms were peeling, which did not help boost my confidence either. It may sound dramatic, but feeling like a nobody at the place where I was once *the* somebody in high school affected me a little more than I wish it had.

I tell you this little story to remind you how important our identity is. Whether we are the "best" or the "worst" in the room at something or seemingly everything, we should still be able to be who we are. Our confidence should not wither simply because we are getting less praise. I believe a lot of people think that as soon as they can do something "big" enough to give them purpose, then they will know their identity or finally feel confident. Let me tell you, when you make the something "big" you can do your purpose, your purpose begins to shrink a whole lot alongside your confidence. Our purpose is to glorify and enjoy God, and when that is the main thing, we are able to see how much bigger our purpose is than success.

Being one of the top sophomore runners in the nation became a lot of my purpose because I got so much praise for it. In my mind, my whole future was determined by how fast I could run someday. Therefore, when it was taken away, pieces of my identity were stripped away, and I did not feel I could have the same confidence if I was not receiving the same praise. The problem with this is I was never the one who was supposed to be receiving the praise. My confidence comes from my posture of praise to the only one who deserves it—God. My prayer for this chapter is that we would silence the voice of the enemy so you can hear the God who shouts to you in your pain. When we decide to believe what God says in His Word about us, and more importantly, about Himself, we can know our identity and live out our purpose, regardless of our feelings or circumstances.

THE SPIRIT IS WILLING, BUT THE FLESH IS WEAK

As believers, we are called "children of light." Paul writes, "For at one time you were darkness, but now you are light in the Lord. Walk as children of light (for the fruit of light is found in all that is good and right and true), and try to discern what is pleasing to the Lord. Take no part in the unfruitful works of darkness, but instead expose them" (Eph. 5:8–11). Dallas Willard explains that to call ourselves children of light is, "in biblical terminology, to say that [we] have the basic nature of light: that light is [our] parent and has passed on to [us] *its* nature, as any parent does."[1]

If you have accepted Jesus into your heart and know God as Father, then your identity is supposed to come from the term *daughter*. You can *know* what God says about you, but what ultimately matters is *who* He is to you. Is He the King of your heart? Because if He is not, no matter how much you know about who He says you are, you will not believe it or identify with it.

Our culture is fascinated with learning about ourselves, with "defining our own truth." We truly are obsessed with ourselves. What if I were to tell you that the real answer to your identity lies in forgetting yourself?

I believe an obvious marker of someone whose identity is in Christ is their thought life. Willard writes:

> Now these people are not perfect and do not live in a perfect world—yet. But they are remarkably different. The difference is not one of a pose they strike, either from time to time or constantly, or of things they do or don't do— though their behavior, too, is very different and distinctive. Where the children of light differ is primarily and most

importantly on the "inside" of their life. It lies in what they are in their depths.

Perhaps the first thing that comes to our attention when we get to know their inner life is what they think about, or what is on their mind. Simply stated, they think about God. He is never out of their mind. They love to dwell up on God and upon his greatness and loveliness, as brought to light in Jesus Christ. They adore him in nature, in history, in his Son, and in his saints. One could even say they are "God-intoxicated" (Acts 2:13; Ephesians 5:18), though no one has a stronger sense of reality and practicality than they do.[2]

I love this passage because it does not guilt trip us about not doing enough for God. It just reminds us how worthy of our obsession He is.

When our mind is full of biblical expressions of who God *is* and His purpose for us in the world, there is not much room for evil to dwell. When we have the heart knowledge of who God is, we are far surer of the enemy's defeat than when we solely have the head knowledge of who God says we are. When we make Jesus, and *His* truth, the King of our heart, we are able to live a life of purpose, knowing our identity. It is far easier to see our identity beyond our feelings when we are not ruled by our feelings because we *know* the truth. You see, as Sadie Robertson Huff shares, "The truth is usually simple until we try to create our own. Normally when we try to create our own truth, we complicate things so much that we forget what the truth even is. When you try to figure out the truth by creating your own truth, you are just distancing yourself from *the truth*, which only leads to more confusion."[3]

The truth that we get to identify with Jesus. Sometimes emotions or circumstances do *feel* like the truth, but that does not mean they are. The stronger we get in our relationship with the

Lord, the more we trust that everything His Word says about us is true because we trust that He Himself is *the* truth. Once we begin to recognize that the loud voices from the enemy and the world are outside are not the truth, it gets a lot easier to silence those voices.

Regarding this battle between *feelings* and the truth, Dallas Willard states:

> And then perhaps we notice—and small wonder given what has already been observed—that the emotional life of these children of light is deeply characterized by love. That is how they invest the emotional side of their being. They love lots of good things and they love people. They love their lives and who they are. They are thankful for their lives—even though it may contain many difficulties, even persecution and martyrdom (Matthew 5:10–12). They receive all of it as God's gift, or at least as his allowance, where they will know his goodness and greatness and go on to live with him forever. And so joy and peace are with them even in the hardest of times—even when suffering unjustly. Because of what they have learned about God, they are confident and hopeful and do not indulge thoughts of rejection, failure, and hopelessness, because *they know better.*[4]

Take a second to think about that phrase, they "do not indulge thoughts of rejection, failure, and hopelessness, because *they know better.*" When I am ever overthinking, upset, or doubting something in life, my husband, Casey, reminds me of just this. He simply says, "Kat, that is not true. I know it feels that way, but you know _____ is true." Sometimes I do not like when he tells me this because it forces me to "man up" and know my identity beyond my feelings. As Matthew 26:41 says, "the spirit is indeed willing, but the flesh is weak." I have accepted Jesus and the Holy Spirit is in me to sing truth over me, but I still have free will to act on or believe certain thoughts and feelings to be true when I know they are not.

"THE LAST OF HUMAN FREEDOMS"

Once we begin this act of stepping into our identity, it looks like surrender after surrender. Similar to what I said in other chapters, nothing necessarily happens overnight, where we instantaneously just *know* exactly what our job and calling is. We do not wake up and suddenly never have to struggle with insecurity around identity again. But we can make it a daily practice to surrender and ask God to continue to show us and take the first seat in our hearts.

I read a story about a man named Viktor Frankl who was an imprisoned Jew in Nazi Germany. He faced unimaginable loss and pain while he was in concentration camps. Both of his parents, his brother, and his wife had all died in the camps from health issues or because they were sent to the gas chambers. He suffered torture and many other horrific events during his time there, never knowing if he would live or die the next day. His situation was hopeless. He had every reason to be miserable and identify with misery and self-pity and let bitterness and hatred of everyone around him take root.

However, one night, he had an epiphany in his dark, bug-infested, sickness-infused bunk. He called it the "last of human freedoms." The "last freedom" meaning one that no one could take away until death:

They could control his entire environment, they could do what they wanted to his body, but Viktor Frankl himself was a self-aware being who could look as an observer at his very involvement. His basic identity was intact. *He could decide within himself how all of this was going to affect him.* Between what happened to him, or the stimulus, and his response to it, was his freedom or power to *choose* that response.[5] (emphasis added)

When we are faced with a stimulus that challenges our identity or, in Viktor's case, our life, we actually have the freedom to choose the response. What a wild idea. What a life-transforming idea that nothing can take away the core of *who I am*—and *who you are*, for that matter. Talk about knowing our identity beyond our feelings. If someone like Viktor Frankl can learn to be strong in who he was when he had every reason to despair, so can we. When all of the dreams of life crash to the floor, as Viktor's clearly had, we still have something we can fall back on. We know, at the core of who we are, regardless of our relationship status, income, family situation, broken dream, or failure, we get to choose our feelings based on knowing our identity. You can pick out your thoughts each morning like you pick out your clothes. You have a choice. It is our responsibility as believers to *believe* God when He tells us He has good plans for our future.

I mentioned in a previous chapter how one of my high school coaches used to always say we should live life "palms up." It is a posture of surrender. If we keep our palms up instead of fists clenched tightly around what we already have, it is much easier to give it up if God asks us to. Then we are already in a position of receiving when He is about to give us something new. I am not telling you to walk around with your palms to the sky all the time.

Do not do that. People will think you are weird. I am simply reminding you that you get the choice to have this heart posture. With this heart posture of, "Lord, this is already Yours anyway, so keep it while I try to steward it well," we are able to ground our identity in what God wants to do through our lives for His glory, not what we want to be successful in through our flesh.

ABIDING OVER STRIVING

When my husband and I first moved to Florida from Georgia, God stirred in my heart to start a Bible study for girls coming out of college. When we first got married, I had just graduated, did not have a job lined up, and was not running in college anymore. I worked at a gym and did a lot of side hustles, plus helped with my husband's company, but I felt devoid of purpose in a lot of ways.

Looking back on that season where I was always so upset about what I was going to "do with my life," I realized I was having a slight identity crisis without knowing it. I loved God, but He was definitely not the only or sole thing giving me purpose. I was lacking all of the busy "doing" I had been used to in college.

At the first meeting of the Bible study, I realized a lot of the girls who had just graduated college felt the same way. I went around the circle of fifteen to twenty new friends and asked what we should do for our study. I asked what things they were currently struggling with that we could learn biblical truth about. Almost every single one of them said they were struggling to know their identity. They said they felt they could only feel accomplished by how much they were getting *done*. One girl discussed how she saw so much of our purpose of resting with God being stripped from us in our culture. The tricky thing about this is when we get our identity and purpose from how much we can *do*, we never take time to actually rest with our Creator to be reminded of our identity and purpose because we are too busy doing.

In reality, our identity has nothing to do with how much we can say or do for God. It has everything to do with what He said and did for us. We are called to be on mission and be busy for the kingdom, but I do not believe we can truly do *damage* for the kingdom if we do not identify first with the Creator of that kingdom. We begin to build our *own kingdom* when we stray from our true identity. You see, one of the reasons Jesus died on the cross for us is because He knew we needed a new identity. He knew we needed a renewed sense of purpose. He knew we needed His help.

When I first started to encounter injuries in high school and could not run, I always got so anxious and struggled with constantly worrying and fretting about my body and future. My dad found a blog post and printed it out and gave it to me. I remember everything that sheet of paper said. It was on abiding instead of striving in life. I had that printed paper for eight years. I would get it out and read it every time I had another injury or painful thing happen in my life. I would bring that sheet and my little pink NIV Bible to a secluded spot in the shade at track meets in high school when I was nervous to run or could not run because of injuries. I would sit with Jesus, read it, and listen to worship music. I would pray and ask God for the strength to trust His plan. I would ask for help to surrender my desire to be an all-American runner again if that was not God's will for me. I would pray for help and peace in trusting God's process.

That simple sheet that said "Abiding Over Striving" and listed a few Scriptures about Jesus' presence with us reminded me who I was and why I was running. Reading that paper took the pressure off me because it reminded me who was actually in control. Reading it allowed me to slow down and be with the one who lights up my soul. The only reason I could be at peace and cheer on my friends—who were able to run pain-free, win races, and set records when I was in so much pain—was because I was *abiding*. I was constantly going back to the one who reminds me who I really am and what really matters in this world.

FOR SUCH A TIME AS THIS

I believe our generation struggles so much with identity because the enemy has gotten us looking at what everyone else is doing instead of looking at our Creator. Looking at everyone else's life makes us more selfish, jealous, and angry because we want what they have. Looking at everyone else makes us more prone to misery because we forget all the good we have. Looking at everyone else makes us forget our identity because we think we have to fit their version of success in order to feel purposeful.

I want to challenge you to go to the one who has all of the answers the next time you feel a twinge of panic over *What will I do for work? What does my future hold?* or *Who am I?* People think identity and purpose are so complicated, but friends, the answer is simple. If your purpose feels heavy, that is because it is. We are on a kingdom assignment, and God wants your help. But how in the world do you think you can help Him if you do not show up for the meeting about your mission?

Our identity does not come from what we do because our identity is who we *are*. And we are daughters in desperate need of some time with our Father. We are daughters who need to be reminded that we are loved, cherished, special, beautifully unique, indispensable, and here on purpose. We figure out our identity when we go to the dictionary of our souls. He wrote your story and created you. Do you not think He knows the definition better than anyone else?

We live out our purpose when we show up for the appointment to ask Him to send us on a mission every day to love as He does. The only way we can do damage and actually get something important done on that mission is if we are abiding, not striving. Not making our dreams an idol and identity is hard because we were made to dream big dreams, work hard for them, and make someone proud.

As I said earlier, the problem arises when we forget whose kingdom we are building, and we have to spend time with the King in order to know how to build the kingdom. Often, when we make our feelings our identity, we are idolizing the way we feel as more important than what God says. Spend some time with your Father and reassess whose kingdom you are building and who you are making proud. He wants to remind you of your identity and mission. He wants you to *know* who you really are and why you are here. Because you are here for a reason and for such a time as this (Est. 4:14)!

7

Celebration Is a Calling

When we go through seasons of waiting and do not feel like any of our dreams are coming true but others' dreams are, it can be hard not to wish for what everyone around us has. I often struggle with comparison when I'm in a waiting season. I think waiting seasons are some of the hardest times not to let bitterness and comparison take over, or just sadness over our wait when we see others seem to easily get what we have prayed for for years.

When Casey and I moved to Florida and I started that Bible study, many of the girls were struggling with knowing their purpose and feeling sad because they were in a waiting season. They were waiting for their dream job or spouse, for a better place to live, a painful situation to end, and so many other things. As we went around the circle sharing our struggles, almost every one of us stated we struggled with comparison when it seemed like everyone else had something better.

One of the best messages I have ever heard on comparison and longing during waiting seasons was at The Grove in Atlanta. It was a women's event hosted by Passion City Church and Shelley

Giglio. Dawn Chere Wilkerson was speaking, and she preached on Psalm 118:24: "This is the day the LORD has made; let us rejoice and be glad in it." She discussed how the psalmist in this verse was actually going through a hard time and it would *not* have been the obvious response for him to be celebrating.[1]

The word *celebrate* means to honor or praise constantly. Celebration does not mean it's a happy day or you got good news; it is rather a discipline that you choose to pick up and build your life with. If we allow ourselves to focus on comparison, no matter how good we have it, we will always feel this sense of discontentment because we are trying to live someone else's life, not our own. But celebrating others is one of the only ways I have found to cripple comparison and beat the enemy at his own game. I believe when we decide to join the psalmist and say, "I will rejoice and be glad in it," because God has me here in this waiting season, we are able to endure much more and cheer others on along the way.

In talking about self-love, author Stephen R. Covey said, "What is self-love is actually self-discipline."[2] What if overcoming comparison does not rely on having some dramatic good thing happen in our lives or having something "better" than others, but is an internal battle? Covey continued:

> Religious leader David O. McKay taught, "the greatest battles of life are fought out daily in the silent chambers of the soul." If you win the battles there, if you settle the issues that inwardly conflict, you feel a sense of peace, a sense of knowing what you're about. And you'll find that the public victories—where you tend to think cooperatively, to promote the welfare and good of other people, and to be genuinely happy for other people's successes—will follow naturally.[3]

I know that, for me, when I activated discipline and asked God to help me cheer on my friends in high school when they were winning state, going to nationals, and doing the things I had loved before my injuries, I was able to be so much more joyful. During our two miscarriages, it took all the strength in me to not want to yell at every mom and pregnant woman around me to stop complaining about motherhood. I'm not judging moms for complaining sometimes. I recognize that mommying is one of the hardest and most important jobs there is! But I wanted to scream how incredibly lucky they were to get to kiss their baby, to rock them to sleep, to be the one who sees them wake up from every nap, and to know what their wailing cry sounds like in the middle of the night.

However, when I allowed myself to feel the anger and rage and bitterness, it did not help my pain at all. If anything, it only made my pain worse because it stopped me from feeling my own sorrow and grieving and led me to anger instead. When I did not activate that discipline of celebration—when I decided to sit in my sorrow and feel bad for myself—I would feel hateful things toward those friends and not want to cheer them on. Just like the situation in a previous chapter where I struggled to be happy for my newlywed friends making their cute houses a home, I would think they should not have the good thing if I could not have it. Many times, when we idolize having or wanting something over God's plan for us, it becomes toxic. This completely makes sense because idolatry, putting anything before God, is a sin and does not lead us to joy!

Dawn Chere Wilkerson discussed this in her message at The Grove. She realized in the middle of her eight-year journey with infertility that she had a choice. She could choose to cower away, be bitter in the wait, and feel hatred toward all of her family and friends who were able to have multiple children before she could conceive—or she could choose celebration. She learned to celebrate and showed up to the baby showers, got the best gifts, and loved her friends a little extra who had kids and needed help. She developed the art and discipline of celebration. Dawn realized it was her calling to say, "This is the day the LORD has made, I will rejoice and be glad in it" (Ps. 118:24). She knew she had a good God, with a good plan. She learned the grit of endurance through the discipline of celebration.

CHARACTER IS WHAT YOU DO
WHEN NOBODY IS WATCHING

Gratitude is also a weapon we oftentimes do not realize we have. I believe gratitude and celebration go hand in hand. If I can be grateful for whatever God is doing in my life, it is going to be much easier to celebrate instead of covet what God is doing in yours.

Dawn Chere Wilkerson also shared how she learned to invest her time in praise. She discovered that she did not need a new circumstance, but a new perspective. Psalm 145:13–21 says:

> Your kingdom is an everlasting kingdom,
>   and your dominion endures throughout all generations,
>   [The LORD is faithful in all his words
>   and kind in all his works.]
> The LORD upholds all who are falling
>   and raises up all who are bowed down.
> The eyes of all look to you,
>   and you give them their food in due season.

You open your hand;
  you satisfy the desire of every living thing.
The LORD is righteous in all his ways
  and kind in all his works.
The LORD is near to all who call on him,
  to all who call on him in truth.
He fulfills the desire of those who fear him;
  he also hears their cry and saves them.
The LORD preserves all who love him,
  but all the wicked he will destroy.
My mouth will speak the praise of the LORD,
  and let all flesh bless his holy name forever and ever.

God opens His hand and satisfies "the desire of every living thing" (v. 16). Remember how we talked about earlier having open hands and living "palms up"? If you offer up your pain and have a posture of praise during it, then God can come and heal your broken heart, because He knows you can hear His voice.

During a season of living with my parents after Casey and I got married, I struggled with wanting what others had because we were not living in the "cute" or "perfect" newlywed setup like I had imagined. I remember when God spoke to me one morning while working at a coffee shop.

Tuesday was my day off, so I set it aside in my calendar as my Sabbath day to rest, stay off my phone more, read, pray, and write a lot. It was such a pretty August day in Georgia, but this particular morning was cooler, which we were thankful for. I put on my mom jeans, purple-embroidered "He Would Love First" crewneck, and checkered Vans with a messy bun. I added a little bit of foundation and some gold hoops, ready to conquer the world one coffee shop at a time.

Once Casey and I got to the coffee shop and sat down, I opened up my Jesus Bible. I had just finished Colossians and was moving right into 1 Thessalonians. My Bible has intros to each book of the Bible and the one before 1 Thessalonians was titled "Give Thanks." I had not been very grateful for my current season and was dealing with comparing myself to a lot of people. After I read the intro and started shifting my heart toward a posture of gratitude, I looked up to think on what I had just read. As soon as I did, the coffee shop wall art in front of me read, "Give thanks." I love when God does that! I started thanking God for things. I thanked Him for my husband across the table from me, my friends who lived in Atlanta, my parents, my experiences, my job, and my car to drive to that job.

While I was reading later that day in 1 Thessalonians 3–4, one of the side notes in my Bible stated this about sanctification: "Sanctification is simply the process of becoming more like God. Believers become more like Him in holiness out of gratitude to God for what He has done in their lives. The Greek word sanctify means to set apart for God's special plans."[4] It is out of a place of gratitude that we see more fully how good God is. Gratitude helps us set ourselves apart for God's special plans. Making the *choice* to be grateful forces us to fix our eyes back on Jesus because we are grateful for the purpose He puts into our pain. In the words of Phillips Brooks:

> Someday, in the years to come, you will be wrestling with the great temptation, or trembling under the great sorrow of your life. But the real struggle is here, now. . . . *Now* it is being decided whether, in the day of your supreme sorrow or temptation, you shall miserably fail or gloriously conquer. Character cannot be made except by a steady, long continued process.[5]

You build your character when you actively decide to celebrate. Just like Dawn Chere Wilkerson celebrated and praised God during her wilderness of eight years of infertility, you get to make that decision as well.

WHAT ARE YOU BUILDING?

One of the most vivid memories I have of this internal struggle of comparison and celebration was my junior year cross-country season when I was going through the peak of some of my health issues. Girls I used to beat by minutes would win the races our team ran. I would get third or fourth, barely limping through the finish line.

In one particular race, when I was dealing with sub-levels of iron and some deficiencies that caused intense fatigue, I ran a time two minutes slower than I had run on that same course when I set the record for it the previous year. I wanted to feel like I had done a good job, but knew I could not run to my potential due to my health. I missed my old self and struggled to tell all of the girls around me who were beating me, "Good job."

I sprinted to the porta-potty immediately after the finish line and cried and prayed a simple prayer. I said, "God, You see this. You know this is hard for me. I know You have made me a good cheerleader. Help me be the best cheerleader out there. Help me genuinely show celebration and joy to these friends. Give me the strength to be a good celebrator because right now I feel too sad, broken, and weak."

Maybe you need to pray that prayer right now too. Maybe you have that person in your life who you just really struggle to champion. It is easy to want to judge or think poorly of someone who has something we want. And that is precisely what the enemy would love—for you to be jealous and discontented. But as believers, celebration should mark our lives.

I want to be someone known for celebrating others. Whatever we are celebrating is what we are building, and we are all building something. So, are you celebrating gossip? Self-pity? Hatred or jealously? Or are you celebrating and building other people's dreams despite your broken ones? Are you celebrating when it's hard? Celebrating when it's hard builds character—good, strong character. Choosing not to celebrate builds character too. It builds bitterness, gossip, and slander. There are only two types of character: good or bad. You choose which one you build.

So, I am challenging you to pray that same prayer I prayed through tears in the porta-potty at a sweaty little cross-country race in high school and am still praying today in the midst of many things. I also am speaking this passage from Ephesians over you:

> Let no corrupting talk come out of your mouths, but only such as is good for building up, as fits the occasion, that it may give grace to those who hear. And do not grieve the Holy Spirit of God, by whom you were sealed for the day of redemption. Let all bitterness and wrath and anger and clamor and slander be put away from you, along with all malice. Be kind to one another, tenderhearted, forgiving one another, as God in Christ forgave you. Therefore, be imitators of God, as beloved children. And walk in love, as Christ loved us and gave himself up for us, a fragrant offering and sacrifice to God. But sexual immorality and all impurity or *covetousness must not even be named* among you, as is proper among saints . . . for at one time you were darkness, but now you are light in the Lord. *Walk as children of*

the light (for the fruit of light is found in all that is good and right and true), and try to discern what is pleasing to the Lord. (Eph. 4:29–5:3, 8–10, emphasis added)

I pray we discern what is pleasing to the Lord and actively choose the discipline of celebration, even when the people walking in the circumstances we are praying for say the wrong thing or are not kind. I pray we can realize what an act of self-love it is to cheer others on even when it is hard.

Jesus is right here, right now, ready to heal you completely before you know if your dream will ever come true or not. It is your decision to celebrate day in and day out. Here's your hug from me and your reminder saying, "I know it hurts, but who can you celebrate during this hurt?" God's Word says, "Those who sow in tears shall reap with shouts of joy!" (Ps. 126:5). During your waiting, allow your tears to be sown so that you will reap shouts of joy. Do not waste your pain, because I promise you God will not.

8

Breathing Dreams Like Air

One time during Bible study, we discussed how to go for big dreams again after we had dreams get broken. To begin, we had everyone go around the circle and say what, as little kids, we wanted to be when we grew up. Then, after we finished going over my notes on dreaming with God, I had each person tell a dream that had been broken or not come true in their life. I shared my running story, and a lot of girls talked about their breakups or family situations. But over half of the group said, "I have never really had a dream. And I think that is the broken part of it because I do not feel very hopeful toward anything in regards to my purpose or calling."

As we continued talking and praying through each of our forms of broken dreams, I shared a story about when Casey and I first got married. I had run in high school and college and been so disappointed and broken by the injuries, and that dream seemed gone. I was not in school anymore and was working a few odd jobs, but nothing I loved. So I felt like I did not have anything I was passionate about to dream for anymore. I remember begging God for another dream, something to wake up for and work hard on every day.

One morning, I was having my quiet time and praying through some of these struggles. As I was asking God for something to dream about, I heard Him say, "You just need Me to be your number one dream. That is all you need right now." After that morning, I still struggled sometimes with feeling a lack of purpose or wanting "my thing," but overall, I struggled a lot less because I would remind myself of what He told me.

As we discussed in earlier chapters, when God is our number one dream, we are in a great position for Him to give us a job or dream to run toward *with* Him. But once we make something else the dream *before* God, it becomes an idol and is no longer healthy. I encouraged each of the girls in the Bible study with this, simply reminding them that Jesus is the number one dream.

We had almost all listed careers when we said our childhood dreams, but dreaming with God is so much more than a job! When we dream with Him, everything else we do flows from that and is *the* dream!

BREATH ON A PAGE

We also had a lot of girls in the Bible study say it was hard for them to dare to dream. They felt like they had never had a massive or broken dream, so they almost felt like their dreams were not big enough. I think this is similar to wanting to dream again after something breaks but being scared to try again and fail.

When we feel like we have nothing to dream for, it is scary even to try because it feels so foreign, like something we do not have access to. I felt this way while in the midst of the injuries and during my time at Baylor. It had been such a long time of fighting against the hard things without stepping back into the fulfillment of my running dreams.

One of the slogans I would constantly repeat to myself is a quote by F. Scott Fitzgerald I found during some late-night Pinterest scrolling. Fitzgerald wrote, "Breathing dreams like air."[1] I loved this phrase because when we wake up in the morning, we breathe without thinking about it. We even breathe all night without having to put a conscious effort in. When I found this quote, waking up daily and doing my rehab, eating healthy, icing my injuries, and going to doctors was all a routine that came naturally to me.

In the Psalms, the psalmist describes with awe and wonder what the Lord has done, stating, "By the word of the LORD the heavens were made, and by the breath of his mouth all their host" (Ps. 33:6). All throughout God's Word, His breath *creates* and breathes life back into dead things, reviving broken dreams, broken families, broken circumstances, and broken people. Breathing life back into our brokenness comes naturally to God. Whether that brokenness is a dream that didn't come true or simply one that has not come into existence yet, He is there to hold and revive our hearts.

When Casey and I walked through our miscarriages, one of my favorite verses was Psalm 34:18, "If your heart is broken, you'll find GOD right there. If you're kicked in the gut, he'll help you catch your breath" (MSG). I loved and clung to this verse because I felt so out of breath like I was fighting for air in that season. I felt more "hope deferred" (Prov. 13:12) than I had ever felt before and needed God's strength and hope to help me catch my breath.

Maybe you've felt that way too. When we see all of the disappointment, bitterness, anxiety, and sadness of our "dark nights" well up in our lives, overwhelming our thoughts, it feels like we cannot breathe. Broken dreams actually feel like suffocation sometimes. Breakups, the death of a loved one, a sickness we never thought we would walk through, betrayal, family hardships—whatever it may be, pain takes our breath away.

The main point of this chapter is to help you get your breath back. So, what does it mean to breathe dreams like air? To dare to dream again after it feels broken?

Life on this side of heaven is not easy, but we have another set of lungs ready to breathe life into us when our hearts get too heavy. One of my favorite messages I have ever heard was at Passion City Church, where Louie Giglio discussed God's Word as His breath on a page.[2] He talked about how God breathed the world into existence in Genesis and how His Word, the Bible, is a continual story of what He breathed into and the truths He breathed out for us to inhale through Scripture. God's Word is not just *His* breath but also how we catch *our* breath. Knowing the truth of God's Word is how we live in a sinking world that feels like we are breathing with no air. Even when we are "underwater" with hard things in a certain season, we can breathe.

Daring to dream again looks like learning how to hope in something worth hoping for. It looks like reaching for God's Word, our life jacket. It looks like committing to memory anthems we can go back to in the midst of some of the worst moments of life when it feels like the enemy wins and there is not much point in picking back up the dream again.

ENGAGING YOUR BREATH AND LUNGS

Being an athlete, I always come up with sports analogies to help myself understand Scripture better because I relate to them.

One of my favorite Scriptures before all of the injuries was Isaiah 40:31. It is very well-known, so you have probably read it, but it states, "But they who wait for the Lord shall renew their strength; they shall mount up with wings like eagles; they shall run and not be weary; they shall walk and not faint."

I used to write this reference on my arm so I could see it in the middle of a race when I wanted to stop pushing the pace and settle for less than my best. When my lungs would start to hurt so badly from pushing myself, I would use this verse to help me push harder. I would look down at my wrist and remember, "I am allowed to ask God for extra strength!" And I would get a new burst of energy to move me forward. My lungs would be hurting just as badly, but I knew who was providing them with the oxygen they needed.

It is the same way with our broken dreams. Your lungs will not necessarily stop hurting. The broken dream might always feel a little broken, and we might not get a full explanation of why things happened the way they did. You might not get the closure you are seeking. But you will be able to turn another page of God's Word. My prayer for you and me is that no matter how great the disappointment we face in this life, no matter how much it feels like we are sinking underwater and we do not know how to get out, we will be able to learn to turn another page, to take another breath.

Being the nerd that I am, I like to look up the original Hebrew or Greek word in the Bible for something and find different places in Scripture where that word is used to get different contextual meanings. The Hebrew word for "breath" is *ruach*. The word *ruach* is not just the Hebrew word for breath but also that of spirit and wind. Commentators say:

When spoken, the word engages one's breath and lungs. The first mention of Ruach in the Bible is in the very first chapter, Genesis 1:2, "And the earth was a formless and desolate emptiness, and darkness was over the surface of the deep, and the Spirit (Ruach) of God was hovering over the surfaces of the waters."[3]

Wow! Can we just take a moment to acknowledge that the first time this word is mentioned is over a formless, desolate, empty, dark, and deep surface (Gen. 1:2)? When our dreams seem broken, dark, or honestly formless because we are not sure what to dream for, we get to breathe the Spirit of God over them. He is always creating a new thing, making beauty out of ashes.

The word *ruach* is also used in the Old Testament in reference to the Spirit of God. Charles Spurgeon writes about the power of the *ruach*'s comfort in sorrow:

> Sometimes, when we go and visit people we mistake their disease, we want to comfort them on this point. Whereas they do not require any such comfort at all, and they would be better left alone than spoiled by such unwise comforters as we are. But oh, how wise the Holy Spirit is! He takes the soul, lays it on the table, and dissects it in a moment; He finds out the root of the matter, He sees where the complaint is. And then He applies the knife where something is required to be taken away or puts a plaster where the sore is. He never mistakes. Oh, how wise, the blessed Holy Ghost! From every comforter I turn and leave them all, for thou art He who alone givest the wisest consolation.[4]

I am someone who wants to come into people's lives and help or "fix" them, if you will. I want to hug you through the pages of this book and say, "Let's be besties. It is all going to be okay." Unfortunately, even if I could do that, it might feel good for a moment. We would feel the comfort of having each other and being there for each other, but I cannot fix you. I cannot even really help you all that much without the help of the ultimate Comforter. And I think that is the crux of daring to dream. We have to be 100 percent dreaming with the King of kings and keeping in line with His timeline and will.

I will be the first person to tell you that God has big dreams for your life, "plans to prosper you and not to harm you, plans to give you a hope and a future" (Jer. 29:11 NIV). No matter your calling, purpose, or the dream you feel called to, if you try to do it without the Comforter and want the dream more than the Dream Giver, there is no comfort. The cure for your exhaustion is intimacy with Jesus. The cure for your deep disappointment occurs when you meet Him in the dark, where it feels too overwhelming, and He begins to overwhelm the overwhelming.

BEAUTIFUL THINGS OUT OF THE DUST

One of the first times I quite literally fell on my face in the dirt in disappointment was in the middle of a "run." I had stopped to walk several times because my legs and injuries just kept hurting beyond the point I could run through. It was back in high school, at the beginning of all the injuries, and if I could have seen the ten-year-plus journey ahead of me, I do not know what I would have thought because even the pain I was in right then seemed too much to handle.

I sat alone in the dirt at the bottom of a steep hill because my teammates had already finished their run. Worship music was quietly coming from my phone, where it sat in the weeds, drowning out my quiet, steady sobs.

With the tears running down my face, I said audibly, not caring if anyone on the trail came by and heard me, "God, You have to make something beautiful out of this. This is dirt. I am sitting in the mud, a sixteen-year-old girl with legs that do not work. I know You are good, and I know You make beautiful things out of the dust. I am sitting here in the dust begging You to make something beautiful out of this because it is far too hard for me to understand and too hard for You to waste." That was in 2015.

In 2022, I helped lead several retreats for girls with body image and disordered eating struggles who were walking through very hard things and very dark seasons. After I shared my testimony and the message God had put on my heart for that weekend, I prayed over the girls that God would make something beautiful out of their dust.

Following the message, as the team led us in worship, I was reminded of that moment in the dirt. It was as if God gave me a hug while I was surrounded by sisters in Christ crying out for beauty in the ashes, and He said, "This is the beautiful. This is what the dirt was for." I wept the rest of the service, and so did most of the girls in the room because of how Jesus was moving.

I tell you this story to say sometimes the "daring to dream" fulfillment, the full circle moment, does not happen for many years. I had to wake up a lot of mornings for new breath. I had to breathe dreams like air. I had to go to Scripture every morning and every dark night. I had to cry out to Jesus over and over and over and plead His presence over my pain. You get to do the same.

God has bigger dreams than we could hope for our lives, but the story is all about Him. What an honor that He invites us in and uses us to help write it! No other version of the story we try to write on our own will be fulfilling or feel like a dream come true because it will be less than we were made for. In Ephesians 4:1, Paul says, "As a prisoner for the Lord, then, I urge you to live a life worthy of the calling you have received" (NIV). Sometimes we just forget to remember *that* is the number one dream come true—that He *chose* us.

THE PRESSURE IS OFF

When I was dealing with my second hip tear, depression, and an eating disorder, the enemy tried to kill my hope by convincing me, "It is always going to be this way." This lie rang loud and clear in my mind 24/7. But, as I mentioned, I loved Fitzgerald's phrase, "breathing dreams like air." It made me take a quick exhale and inhale to remember that God could turn my life around, and I could find joy again. I could find strength to dream again if I just remembered to breathe and let go of the fear that "it might always be this way."

I shared this in previous chapters, but some of the most crucial parts of my story were formed from learning how to dream big dreams again, thinking through my passions and interests with God, and assessing the best way to follow *His* lead into those things. I think sometimes we are scared to dream big, not only because we believe things will never change but because we do not want to embarrass ourselves. But in reality, if our dreams and future are in God's hands, it takes the pressure off us or how it will make us look because it is all about glorifying Him, not us.

We still have to work hard toward our dreams, but we do not have to measure our success the same way the world does!

We get to replace what we might have settled for with what we have been longing for—a lasting sense of purpose with God in the right place. This allows our ambition to continue to grow toward chasing our dreams in a healthy way.

Sometimes, we also need a little reminder about how dark it looked in Genesis 1 before light was created, and before God's breath breathed our lives onto the page. Breathing dreams like air requires day-by-day learning to love and live like the one who provides the oxygen that this world cannot.

9

Eyes Fixed

A while back, I was stressed about a few areas of my life. We had been out of town for almost a month, helping with some family things, and had a lot going on. I was about to go speak at an event and had just twisted my ankle on a run. I felt a bit bummed about it and my injuries overall because I had been working really hard and seeing progress in physical therapy. It all seemed to be going downhill now. I was trying to be positive and just know that I would keep working hard and it would all work out.

In that season of my life, we were trying for a baby, so I almost felt guilty anytime I got busy or stressed with life things because I knew it was not good for my hormones or fertility to be stressed. I would have people tell me just to quit doing the things that stressed me out. They didn't mean it to come off as belittling, but it did because I had been working really hard with my running, speaking, book, and some private goals. I felt passion and purpose behind everything I was doing and knew God was calling me to work hard, even if it was stressful at times.

I think that when it comes to goals or hard things God calls us to, a lot of people have thoughts like the ones people shared with me during this time. These thoughts are a big reason many of them do not pursue the things God is calling them to do. They think it might be too stressful. To some degree, yes, it is good to eliminate unnecessary stress in our lives, but sometimes, we just need to learn how to manage that stress better!

When Casey and I first moved to Florida, I got some prophetic words about running again at churches and events from people who did not even know my history with the sport. I asked God if I was allowed to pursue running again and felt Him calling me to work hard toward distance running. I did not think I would go pro or do anything crazy. I just knew I was allowed to pursue something I loved again.

But I knew God was calling me also to say yes to things I did not know how to do, and I learned to lean into trust, knowing I could have peace that He would do it on my behalf. For example, I had found anxiety and stress in the past whenever I was asked to speak at events because speaking terrified me. My verse around these stressful or scary things in life became Isaiah 41:10. It says, "Fear not, for I am with you; be not dismayed, for I am your God; I will strengthen you, I will help you, I will uphold you with my righteous right hand." This verse helped calm my stress and fear because God was saying He would be the one to physically "uphold" me when I did not know what to say, when I fell and hurt myself on a run, or when anything stressful in life happened. When I was "dismayed" or stressed, His hand was the one that would bring me peace in the midst of the season or battle.

There might be areas in your life you have heard others or your own voice say, "That is too stressful for me." It might seem like that "off-limits" thing you could never do, but you feel a tug toward, is too hard. But is it too hard for God?

I remember assessing what my friends said because sometimes we need to cut unnecessary stressors and unneeded things out of our lives. Yet, if we know something is a call from God, we need to learn to do the opposite. We need to learn to say yes at all costs and ask God to teach us how to pray for peace when everything around us just seems like a problem. I think that is one of the coolest parts of doing things that challenge our faith—we learn to see how small the problems we view as stressful and impossible are because we have a big God.

BY FAITH

When you picked up this book, you read the subtitle, *Fixing Our Eyes on Jesus in the Midst of Broken Dreams.* We have heavily discussed this theme, but as we begin to come to a close in these last two chapters, I want to continue to dive into Hebrews 11–12, along with what it means to fix our eyes on Jesus in the midst of hard things He calls us to do. Sometimes the hard thing is trusting Him in the broken dream and surrendering it. However, other times it is having the courage and discipline to either reignite a dream or pursue a new one with Him. Either way, and with anything we tackle in life, if our eyes aren't "fixed," then life will end up feeling and being broken!

As we talked about in an earlier chapter, Hebrews 11 is the "by-faith greats" section of the Bible. Some of these "greats" are listed for their faithfulness through hard work, having faith during broken dreams, or believing in promises that seemed like they were far off and forgotten. But some of them were also people who had faith in the waiting seasons and then the faith to act when God said to. Even when they did not feel like they were enough to do the thing they were asked to by God:

- "By faith Moses, when he had grown up, refused to be known as the son of Pharaoh's daughter. He chose to be mistreated along with the people of God rather than to enjoy the fleeting pleasures of sin" (Heb. 11:24–25 NIV).
- "By faith the walls of Jericho fell, after the army had marched around them for seven days" (Heb. 11:30 NIV).
- "By faith Abraham, when called to go to a place he would later receive as his inheritance, obeyed and went, even though he did not know where he was going" (Heb. 11:8 NIV).

The list goes on, where people did things even if they were hard or stressful and did not make sense to themselves or those around them. There was a still, small voice in the midst of them, guiding them, reminding them where their courage and peace came from.

Worry and fear are universal. Pretty much anyone you meet has encountered them. When stress comes, most of us run to some form of medication. I do not necessarily mean medication as in medicine, more in the form of a distraction or addiction. I want to discuss three ways in which we can keep calm and shine our light even in the midst of adversity and distractions.

1. Know Who You Are and Who You Are Chosen By

We have discussed identity a decent amount in these pages, and Scripture calls us children of God if we believe in Him. Therefore, you are a child of God and He *chose* you to be His child because He loves you and has a plan for you. You have to know you are chosen or you will not be able to walk out God's plan for you in your "such a time as this" moments (see the book of Esther).

We all have moments and seasons in life where we have to choose to believe we are chosen. If we do not, then the task in front of us seems too hard. When you simply think you are "choosing" to do something, instead of knowing that you were chosen by God to do that thing, it is much harder to believe and take action. In those cases, we are believing in ourselves and relying on temporary motivation instead of God's voice.

The first year or so of speaking, when an event seemed too hard and scary, I was not remembering who chose me to speak into those young girls' lives. When I had anxiety attacks months before speaking somewhere, I was choosing to believe the enemy's lies that I did not have what it takes, instead of believing that God would reach out His hand and strengthen, confirm, and establish me while on that stage if I was doing it as unto Him. I want you to sit back and reflect on how you feel chosen. Also, think about the areas of your life you do not believe in your identity as a daughter who was chosen by her Father.

When Jesus decided to die on the cross and raise from the dead for you, He did something stressful. He literally sweated blood the night before because He was so heavily grieving the hard thing God was asking Him to do. He even begged His Father to take the task away from Him. But ultimately, Jesus knew it was the Father's will and He was chosen—the only one to fulfill God's plan to save me and you. The cost of us not choosing to know we are chosen by the God who died for us, is a lot more costly than we might think. The cost of choosing the thing we were chosen for is worth the stress, friend.

2. Remember That the Holy Spirit Is with You

The second fact we need to remember when beating stressful areas in our life is that we carry the Holy Spirit. If you are a believer, then the Light of the World dwells inside of you. With the power of the Holy Spirit within us comes a helper when we need it most. First Thessalonians 1:5 says, "Because our gospel came to you not simply with words but also with power, with the Holy Spirit and deep conviction. You know how we lived among you for your sake" (NIV). I believe one of the convictions we carry is not to live our lives full of stress and anxiety even when doing hard things. We carry the power and the peace of the Holy Spirit within us, and we get to tap into that. We have to be humble enough to say it is stressful and we cannot do it without Him!

We also carry the conviction to do the stressful things. When we pray prayers like, "God, break my heart for what breaks Yours," are we actually asking Him to do that? Because with the Holy Spirit inside of us, we *will* feel those heart pulls and, if it breaks our heart enough, maybe we will have the courage to take action on it.

I believe we are all called to ministry. Whether it be starting a physical ministry, speaking, your nine-to-five job, working as a waitress, or whatever you do, you have the Holy Spirit in you, so you have the conviction of living your life doing ministry. Paul says in 2 Corinthians:

> Therefore, since through God's mercy we have this ministry, we do not lose heart. . . . For what we preach is not ourselves, but Jesus Christ as Lord, and ourselves as your servants for Jesus' sake. For God, who said, "Let light shine out of darkness," made his light shine in our hearts to give us the light of the knowledge of God's glory displayed in the face of Christ.

But we have this treasure in jars of clay to show that
this all-surpassing power is from God and not from us.
We are hard pressed on every side, but not crushed; per-
plexed, but not in despair; persecuted, but not abandoned;
struck down, but not destroyed. We always carry around
in our body the death of Jesus, so that the life of Jesus may
also be revealed in our body. (2 Cor. 4:1, 5–10)

This Scripture is such a picture of what it looks like to live
chosen, carrying around the knowledge and conviction that you
have been made new to declare "let light shine out of darkness"
(v. 6). That is the power we carry, the most important thing
about us. I think one of the top things young adults, and maybe
all of us, are confused about is what our job should be or what
our purpose is. Yes, you can find so much calling and purpose
in your job, but your real purpose comes from the one inside
you and deciding to live your life in ministry even when the
world isn't.

3. You Are No Longer a Slave to Fear

So, you are a chosen child of God and you have asked Jesus
to come into your heart and you believe He died for you. Most
of us have all of that as head knowledge but maybe not as heart
knowledge quite yet. But once you begin to live in relation with
Jesus, where you talk to Him, get to know Him, you can live out
1 Thessalonians 1:6. It says, "You became imitators of us and of
the Lord, for you welcomed the message in the midst of severe
suffering with the joy given by the Holy Spirit (NIV)." Paul in
his letter to the Thessalonians is saying: *See, you are fearless! Even
in the midst of great suffering you could lean on the joy of the Holy
Spirit that you carry!*

This leads me to the third point I wanted to bring up. The reason we can live with healthy stress in our lives during hard things or challenging callings is that we are no longer slaves to fear! Romans 8:15 says, "For you did not receive the spirit of slavery to fall back into fear, but you have received the Spirit of adoption as sons, by whom we cry, 'Abba! Father!'" Realizing we are chosen, believing who God says we are, and "wearing" the Holy Spirit by putting on the armor of God—through realizing that He is with us and fighting on our behalf—is what allows us to stomp on fear's head. So yes, anxiety and stress might pop up in our lives through the things God calls us to, but He steadies us with the constant reminder that we are no longer slaves to fear, but we are children of God.

Living as children of God sets us apart because we are called to be lights to the world. But sometimes being a light is stressful because you stand out in the dark. You stand up for biblical truth and are called to look different. Sometimes looking different means still having hope in the midst of a very dark season. Sometimes it looks like having joy when no one else would in your current season. We are allowed to mourn; we are allowed to be busy. We are allowed to acknowledge we are human and the things God calls us to aren't easy, but as 2 Corinthians 4:13–18 (NIV) says:

> Since we have that same spirit of faith, we also believe and therefore speak, because we know that the one who raised the Lord Jesus from the dead will also raise us with Jesus and present us with you to himself. All this is for your benefit, so that the grace that is reaching more and more people may cause thanksgiving to overflow to the glory of God.
>
> Therefore we do not lose heart. Though outwardly we are wasting away, yet inwardly we are being renewed day by

day. For our light and momentary troubles are achieving for us an eternal glory that far outweighs them all. So we fix our eyes not on what is seen, but on what is unseen, since what is seen is temporary, but what is unseen is eternal.

I love how verse 16 says "day by day" because we do have to remind ourselves daily to decide to not let ourselves be a slave to fear. We have to decide how we handle our daily stressors and the things the Lord calls us to. Do we respond with hope and grace, seasoned with the discernment of the Holy Spirit, or do we respond like the rest of the world?

WHEN WE GET GRATEFUL, WE GET GOOD

As we begin to close out this chapter, I want to go back to Hebrews 11–12 again. The subtitle of this book and of many of our lives is *Fixing Our Eyes on Jesus in the Midst of Broken Dreams*, and Hebrews 12:1–3 (NIV) states:

Therefore, since we are surrounded by such a great cloud of witnesses, let us throw off everything that hinders and the sin that so easily entangles. And let us run with perseverance the race marked out for us, fixing our eyes on Jesus, the pioneer and perfecter of faith. For the joy set before him he endured the cross, scorning its shame, and sat down at the right hand of the throne of God. Consider him who endured such opposition from sinners, so that you will not grow weary and lose heart.

What we just read in 2 Corinthians also says this as well—we need to daily fix our eyes. I know we had a whole chapter about faith earlier and what it means to have faith, so you might feel like an expert in the faith department by now. But the reality is, the only way we grow in our faith is by fixing our eyes on the Author of it. And yes, as we talked about, trust is the action of faith, but I believe it is also the action of setting our gaze on God. The action of saying, "I choose to look at You, God, during this race called life. Even when I get out of breath and I want to look to my right or left or down at my feet and take a walking break, instead I'm going to look up again, toward the finish line." That is the way we live fearless, that is the way we grow faith and have perseverance.

As we pursue our endeavors and go about our callings, walking in God's purpose in our lives, we are to view it as Jesus did the cross—as the joy set before us that Hebrews 12 talks about. In the NIV, the last headline in Hebrews 12 is, "The Mountain of Fear and the Mountain of Joy." In the ESV, it says, "A Kingdom That Cannot Be Shaken." Mount Zion in these passages is a picture of a new heavenly Zion or Jerusalem. It is a symbol to say we have access to a spiritual realm—a heavenly Jerusalem—and we get to "participate in worship with innumerable angels" and other "greats" in heaven.[1] That is our eternal inheritance because, once again, we are *chosen* and now children.

Hebrews 12:28–29 states, "Therefore let us be grateful for receiving a kingdom that cannot be shaken, and thus let us offer to God acceptable worship, with reverence and awe, for our God is a consuming fire." Gratitude has become such a fad in our culture because truly, when we get grateful, we get good! We are able to see more clearly everything we go through when we channel it through a lens of gratitude. And when our lens is on heaven, yes, we are allowed to mourn the hard things of this earth but we have an unshakable eternity to set our gaze on and remember that we have so much to be grateful for.

WE "PROTECT OUR PEACE"
BY KNOWING PEACE HIMSELF

Something else that is also a huge fad in our culture and generation is the slogan, "Protect Your Peace." I understand this saying to some degree, but the context it is most typically used in on social media or secular magazines is to block anything out of your life that does not "serve you." However, as believers, that goes against the grain of everything we are called to. In discussing Christ's example of humility, Paul states:

> Do nothing from selfish ambition or conceit, but in humility count others more significant than yourselves. Let each of you look not only to his own interests, but also to the interests of others. Have this mind among yourselves, which is yours in Christ Jesus, who, though he was in the form of God, did not count equality with God a thing to be grasped, but emptied himself, by taking the form of a servant, being born in the likeness of men. (Phil. 2:3–7)

If we really want to "protect our peace," we get close to the one who brought peace on earth and good will to men. Ephesians 2:14 says, "For He Himself is our peace, who has made both one, and has broken down the middle wall of separation" (NKJV). We protect our peace by returning to our Master's side. When we are serving God, doing the tasks we are called to with the help of the Holy Spirit and doing them for and with Him the entire time, we also get to return to a state of rest in His presence. And that is where we get to know peace. We do not necessarily "protect" it, but we get more of it by trusting and staying close to our Father.

If you are anything like me, as soon as something really good happens in life, you immediately start to worry whether it will be taken away or if something else bad will happen. But when we are walking with Jesus, this stress and anxiety of the "what ifs" may still be there, but they are met with assurance that the definition and presence of peace Himself is right there with us. Therefore, no matter the outcome, how long the wait, or how bad the diagnosis, we can have peace in the midst of the sorrow.

I know it is hard to wrap our minds around this, but the more we get to know God's character and the unshakeable eternity we get to fix our gaze on, the easier it is to believe in the possibility of peace and grace in the midst of anxiety and sorrow. One of the names of the Holy Spirit is Comforter/Helper (John 14:26). He should be our comforter, not the worldly peace we receive from good circumstances in our lives. When our lives are focused solely on our own peace and how we can "protect" it, instead of having our eyes fixed on the Prince of Peace, we cannot live out much of our purpose.

God might call you to do some stressful things, but He will never leave your side. He continually will be there holding your hand and calling you to set your gaze on the things that matter. When your heart is in the right place, your head usually follows. Fixing your eyes on Jesus and knowing peace Himself is the best way to protect your peace and fulfill your purpose in this life.

10

When It Feels Like Things Can't Get Much Worse

January 6, 2023, around 3 p.m., I got home from an appointment and noticed Casey was out running some errands, so I had the house to myself. We had been trying for our first baby for about a year, and I was pretty accustomed to my period just starting and informing me that there would be no baby that month. However, this time I was a day or two late and had an opportunity to take a test very quickly before Casey got home.

I ran into the bathroom and set up my little vlog camera. I had set it up so many times before when I had taken pregnancy tests, so I could record a sweet and happy reaction whenever that day came. Fully expecting the test to be negative, I covered the test up for the three minutes the instructions tell you to wait for. Before looking at the test, I held it up to my camera for the "vloggers" to see, and out of the corner of my eye, I saw a reflection of the test in the mirror, and I gasped. The wait was over.

Tears immediately streamed to my eyes, and prayers of "Thank You, God! Thank You, Lord," came out between the sobs of joy. But what I did not know was that the wait was not over—a much harder wait was just about to start.

At around eleven weeks, I was at the emergency room at ten o'clock at night, miscarrying and laboring with our firstborn. Just a few short months later, we miscarried again. After eighteen months of praying for our baby, we had two in heaven and none on earth.

If you have been through a season of grief so deep you don't really know how you will be able to breathe again, then you know how I felt in the spring of 2023. My world came crashing down over and over. The thrill of seeing a positive pregnancy test I had waited for all those months seemed somehow tainted now. I remember during the intense period of sadness following the first miscarriage, I almost never stopped crying. I felt empty, numb, and depleted of everything good.

However, these days had me dreaming, not just longing for but almost living for the thought of going to heaven. Losing the babies I dreamed of, carried, and never got to meet creates a longing and heartbreak that will never fully pass, no matter how much "time heals." I remember thinking of the previous chapter on Hebrews 11–12. I had written it just weeks before our first baby left us to be with Jesus, and I thought, "Wow. I thought I knew how to fix my eyes and long for heaven *then*, but now . . ." I have never ached so heavily to go to a place before. My longing to meet my babies and stop experiencing the pains of this earthside life ate at me like nothing had before. I was continually reminded that this place is not my home, and I thank God for that. I was forcefully reminded where my eyes should be fixed and where my true and only source of hope comes from.

CATCHING YOUR BREATH

People always say God is near to the brokenhearted because of Psalm 34:18. I shared it in an earlier chapter, but as a reminder, it states, "If your heart is broken, you'll find GOD right there; if you're kicked in the gut, he'll help you catch your breath" (Ps. 34:18 MSG). If you are currently living in that "gut punch," but you haven't been able to catch your breath yet, I am with you.

It is all good and well for me to write another sweet "trust God" and "fix your eyes on heaven" book to remind us of biblical truths. But it is another thing for me to sit here and say, "I get it. I am broken into pieces and shattered on the floor right now too." I am not perfect. After the second miscarriage, there were a few days where for the first time in my life I could say I felt mad at God.

There were several things going on other than the first miscarriage before we were surprised by the second pregnancy and then devastated by the second miscarriage. I remember begging God for relief. Before the second pregnancy even came into existence, I was on my knees asking God to make things good again because there was more "bad" going on than I had ever experienced. Family, marriage, work issues, ministry, and my health post-miscarriage, among other things, felt like they were all about to make me implode into a fury of grief, sorrow, and rage.

I had never felt mad at God before. And I was realizing even though I thought I was angry at Him this time, I was really just offended. My prayers felt like a broken "I trusted You! I know You are good, and I trusted You with this, so how are You allowing this?! Father, how on earth is this what You call 'good'?" I know most of us have those big questions in our life where we may ask, "How could a good God allow *this* bad thing?"

During the miscarriages and just the overall hardship of that spring, I would try to reason in my head why God was doing this or that and attempt to make sense of it somehow. I know God is in everything and writes our stories, so oftentimes, I try to predict why He is telling the story a certain way. One day, after the first appointment and ultrasound that told us we had most likely miscarried the second pregnancy, I was trying to explain to Casey how I really didn't understand what God was doing.

He stopped me and said, "Listen, Kat. I know God uses things in our stories and is in them, but you have got to quit overthinking every single thing that happens to us as 'God doing it.' The reality is that, yes, God uses things that happen to us and makes them good, but also things just happen in life—crazy things. And it is not necessarily because God willed it to happen to teach you something."

One of the books that brought me the most wisdom and comfort in the weeks following our first disappointment and loss was *A Grief Observed* by C. S. Lewis. In the introduction, Douglas H. Gresham talks about the book and Lewis's emotions. He states, "This book is a man emotionally naked in his own Gethsemane. It tells of the agony and the emptiness of a grief such as few of us have to bear, for the greater the love the greater the grief, and the stronger the faith the more savagely will Satan storm its fortress."[1] One of the passages in the first chapter that spoke to my mourning momma's heart and I hope speaks to yours, no matter what type of loss or hardship you might be facing, is as follows:

> And poor C. quotes to me, "Do not mourn like those that
> have no hope." It astonishes me, the way we are invited
> to apply to ourselves words so obviously addressed to our
> betters. What St. Paul says can comfort only those who love

God better than the dead, and the dead better than themselves. If a mother is mourning not for what she has lost but
for what her dead child has lost, it is a comfort to believe
that the child has not lost the end for which it was created.
And it is a comfort to believe that she herself, in losing her
chief or only natural happiness, has not lost a greater thing
that she may still hope to "glorify God and enjoy Him
forever." A comfort to the God-aimed, eternal spirit within
her. But not to her motherhood. The specifically maternal
happiness must be written off. Never in any place or time,
will she have her son on her knees, or bathe him, or tell him
a story, or plan for his future, or see her grandchild.[2]

Lewis goes on to describe the pain and grief and heavy loss
he experienced when he lost his wife to cancer. He jots down
thoughts about his questioning whether God can even be described as "good." In his initial chapters, he compares God to a
dentist throughout the process in the sense that God is there to
fix what is broken, and it can hurt. But God is not the one creating the problem. He is simply the one trying to fix it. Regarding
this internal battle he felt, Lewis states:

The more we believe that God hurts only to heal, the less
we can believe there is any use in begging for tenderness.
A cruel man might be bribed—might grow tired of his vile
sport—might have a temporary fit of mercy, as alcoholics
have fits of sobriety. But suppose that what you are up
against is a surgeon whose intentions are wholly good. The
kinder and more conscientious he is, the more inexorably
he will go on cutting. If he yielded to your entreaties, if he
stopped before the operation was complete, all the pain
up to that point would have been useless. But is it credible

that such extremities of torture should be necessary for us? Well, take your choice. The tortures occur. If they are unnecessary, then there is no God or a bad one. If there is a good God, then these tortures are necessary. For not even a moderately good Being could possibly inflict or permit them if they weren't.[3]

Perhaps we are often crying and screaming so loud in the midst of the heaviest hardships that we are all but blocking from our hearts God's tender words. I will be the first to tell you it was hard to hear God during the pain of miscarriage. I felt His peace and presence but it was all but impossible to hear His whisper in that "dark night."

HE'S IN THE DETAILS

I reference this "dark night" fairly often as I have talked about hard things throughout these pages we have shared together, and that is because no matter how good our life gets, there will always be hard things marked with "darkness." As Gresham states regarding Satan, "The stronger the faith the more savagely will Satan storm its fortress."[4] Before sin and brokenness had even entered mankind, the enemy was already fighting to put a barrier between us and God. And then the second Adam and Eve sinned, our world became broken, which was just beginning of those dark nights for humanity.

If you are new to your faith or haven't read Genesis in the Bible, this would be a great place to start. Essentially, Adam and Eve listened to the lies of Satan about whether or not God's decree for them were good and true. What happened in the garden of Eden in Genesis 2–3, where Adam and Eve chose

Satan's whispers over God's way, is still to this day the reason we face dark nights. From that moment on, not only sin but brokenness entered the perfect world God had created. I have mentioned it before in a previous chapter, but the season we are living in can be described as an awkward in-between because we aren't in the garden of Eden and we aren't in heaven yet.[5] You and I are still in the brokenness.

However, there was an event in history that changed the direction of this brokenness. We are in the awkward in-between of this dark and hard world, but we now get to live in relation with the one who is more than able. We now have access to the Holy Spirit. In the garden of Eden, when God finished creating man and woman, He validated that it is was very good (Gen. 1:31), and rested on the seventh day. Unfortunately, as we just discussed above, it did not stay "good" for very long.

After the fall, there was a separation between us and God as soon as Adam and Eve sinned. But now we are not separated anymore. It says in Matthew 27 that the curtain in the temple, which used to separate the holy of holies from anyone who came to pray, ripped in half as Jesus died on the cross:

From noon until three in the afternoon darkness came over all the land. About three in the afternoon Jesus cried out in a loud voice, *"Eli, Eli, lema sabachthani?"* (which means "My God, my God, why have you forsaken me?"). . . . And when Jesus had cried out again in a loud voice, he gave up his spirit. At that moment the curtain of the temple was torn in two from top to bottom. The earth shook, the rocks split and the tombs broke open. The bodies of many holy people who had died were raised to life. (Matt. 27:45–46, 50–52 NIV)

I love that God does not forget any details. Sometimes we forget the details. We know Jesus died on the cross for our sins. We often take it for granted and should never cease to be in awe of it. Even more often, we forget the detail of the curtain in the temple, or the "veil" as Scripture calls it, ripping in two once He dies and says, "It is finished" (John 19:30).

As I write these closing words on the closeness of our Father due to the cross, it is Easter weekend and I am adamantly reminded how beautiful the story of death and resurrection is. This year is our first season living in Florida, and the spring comes sooner here. The air has been warmer, brighter, and more hopeful, even in the midst of miscarriages and hardship. I texted my mother this morning, as she has encouraged me during this writing process, and said, "It is wild that I am finishing the last chapter of the book, trying to put hope and truth to the chapter that is on my previous miscarriage, when I am currently physically miscarrying my second time."

I have had trouble wanting to "do ministry" right now—to write or speak or care about spreading hope—because I have moments where I feel hopeless in my own circumstances. One of the harder feelings that came with the miscarriage was a numbness, an apathy almost. I lost interest in anything I loved because I was hurting so deeply it felt like nothing much mattered. My house was a mess, I did not want to eat, I was physically sick from the miscarriages, so I could not move my body or enjoy the fact that we lived less than a mile from the beach.

However, the timing of the second miscarriage happened to fall so closely to Good Friday and Easter weekend. It was a forced and much needed reminder that He, the Author and Perfector of our faith, is very acquainted with sorrow. In Scripture, it says:

He was despised and rejected by mankind,
  a man of suffering, and familiar with pain.
Like one from whom people hide their faces
  he was despised, and we held him in low esteem.
Surely he took up our pain
  and bore our suffering,
yet we considered him punished by God,
  stricken by him, and afflicted.
But he was pierced for our transgressions,
  he was crushed for our iniquities;
the punishment that brought us peace was on him,
  and by his wounds we are healed. . . .
By oppression and judgment he was taken away.
  Yet who of his generation protested?
For he was cut off from the land of the living;
  for the transgression of my people he was punished.
He was assigned a grave with the wicked,
  and with the rich in his death,
though he had done no violence,
  nor was any deceit in his mouth. (Isaiah 53:3–5, 8–9 NIV)

What a wild concept that He went through all of this to comfort you and me. And how often do we run to other comforts such as scrolling, addiction, or comparison instead of going "beyond the veil" and entering into His presence—the place He died for?

As believers, we celebrate Good Friday and the cross because of what it means and what God did. We feel the heaviness of His sacrifice and our *need* for this sacrifice. And then there's the Saturday during Easter weekend. It is a day of brokenness over Friday, the cross, and Jesus' death. It is a period of grief and broken dreams that feels like a desperate in-between. However, for us, Saturday isn't hopeless. It is also filled with hope and long-ing because we know Sunday and the resurrection are coming.

In many ways, I think grief over something broken, like a loss, can feel like that Saturday. Yet we have hope that others do not have because we know God is good even when our cir-cumstances are not. We know there is hope for the Sunday that is coming because we know He already won all our battles and rose from the dead. God is not just good to the point of dying for us, but to the point of sending His Holy Spirit to be with us.

Your tears are not in vain. This season you are in is hard, and that is validated. During your season of tears, Jesus honors the brokenness and sits with you. And having Jesus enter into your pain allows you to lean into learning how to further rely on Him. And when He comes and sits with you, He helps you fix your eyes on Sunday. He will resurrect you, friend. You need only fix your eyes. Your resurrection is coming.

LOOKING FOR EVIDENCE

Casey and I live in the cutest little beach town neighborhood, and one of my favorite things about our cozy house is that we can walk to a little coffee shop on the corner of our street. As soon as I found out I was pregnant (both times), and even while we were trying to conceive, I dreamed of walking with a stroller to this coffee shop and the park down the road from us too.

The first few weeks, especially after the first miscarriage, go-ing to these spots felt sad because a dream felt like it was miss-ing. However, if you had told little Kathryn and Casey who got married three years ago and lived with my parents in the middle of nowhere that we would live in the cutest beach town and walk to coffee every Saturday from our adorable house, we wouldn't have believed you. We were standing in one answered prayer and fulfilled dream, while another was breaking.

My offering to myself and you through sharing this story is to remind us to realize the fullness the Lord is offering in the answered prayers we are currently walking in while we wait for the broken dreams to be mended. Fixing our eyes on Him—and on heaven—is really the only way to be in awe of all the good in the midst of the brokenness here on earth. There is good all around us; it just feels impossible to see it sometimes.

The last note I want to leave you with as we close this book is that of the nearness of God throughout your whole story. There are certain people and role models I look up to in life. They all have one thing in common: they are very good at seeing God's faithfulness because they are near to Him.

Have you ever heard a testimony that just blows you away and leaves you in awe? I have heard many, and most of them are stunningly beautiful not just because you can see God's faithfulness in the end result, but because you saw His faithful hand there the whole time. Throughout the whole story, He still had the pen in His hand and left no room for error.

When I actually reside in a slow enough pace to listen in and ask God for more answers, He does not tell me the why behind something happening, but He will speak to me. I have been asking Him like never before to be near to me in this season of loss and heartache.

Your and my story are the same in the sense that He is writing them and He is a much better Storyteller, Future Planner, and Author than any of us could ever be. I just sat in bed crying a few weeks ago before falling asleep because I had seen God's faithfulness in my waiting season in so many special ways. However, I wasn't crying over His goodness, but my lack of it.

I knew I would have seen His faithfulness in my story so much more if I had been more faithful to listening and learning along the way. When we lean into the waiting, when we ask Him for sweet reminders along the way, He gives them. We can look for evidence of what He is doing all along.

I am leaning "further up and further in,"[6] while fixing my eyes on heaven. I am asking for more sweet reminders throughout my day that no matter how bad it gets I can still see His goodness in the land of the living. I will leave you with 2 Corinthians 4:16–18:

> So we do not lose heart. Though our outer self is wasting away, our inner self is being renewed day by day. For the light momentary affliction is preparing for us an eternal weight of glory beyond all comparison, as we look not to the things that are seen but to the things that are unseen. For the things that are seen are transient, but the things that are unseen are eternal.

God has so much for your story—so much He considered it worth dying for. Do not give up, friend. Keep your head up and your heart strong. I am praying that this book and these words give you fresh wind in your sails and the confidence to dream again. No matter how many dreams get broken in this broken world, Jesus will always be there waiting to remind us He is our number one dream. Here is to breathing dreams like air! May you give your lowest for His highest.

Notes

CHAPTER 1: A FATHER'S LOVE

1. C. S. Lewis, *The Magician's Nephew* (New York: HarperCollins, 1983), 168.
2. Hannah Hurnard, *Hinds' Feet on High Places* (Summit, NJ: Start Publishing LLC, 2013), chap. 1, https://www.google.com/books/edition/Hinds_Feet_on_High_Places/Q1PsAgAAQBAJ?hl=en&gbpv=1.

CHAPTER 2: WHEN A DREAM GETS BROKEN

1. Janet and Geoff Benge, *Eric Liddell: Something Greater than Gold* (Seattle, WA: YWAM Publishing, 1998).
2. Lysa TerKeurst, *It's Not Supposed to Be This Way: Finding Unexpected Strength When Disappointment Leaves You Shattered* (Nashville: Thomas Nelson, 2018).
3. A. W. Tozer, *The Pursuit of God* (Grand Rapids: Baker Publishing Group, 2013), 40.
4. Ibid., 41.
5. Bob Goff, *Dream Big: Know What You Want, Why You Want It, and What You're Going to Do About It* (Nashville: Nelson Books, 2020), 163.
6. Tozer, *The Pursuit of God*, 42.

CHAPTER 3: LIVING IN THE DARK NIGHT

1. C. S. Lewis, *The Screwtape Letters* (New York: HarperCollins, 1942), 67.

2. "Understanding Gen Z Report 2019," Morning Consult Pro, June 2019, https://morningconsult.com/form/gen-z-report-download/.
3. Lydia Price, "Celeb Confessions That'll Make You Never Want to Be Famous," *People*, April 12, 2021, https://people.com/celebrity/celeb-confessions-that-will-make-you-never-want-to-be-famous/.

CHAPTER 4: LEARNING HOW TO HEAL

1. Katherine and Jay Wolf, *Hope Heals: A True Story of Overwhelming Loss and an Overcoming Love* (Grand Rapids: Zondervan, 2020).
2. Katherine Wolf, shared in a message at Hope Heals Camp, July 16, 2019.
3. C. S. Lewis, *The Last Battle* (New York: HarperTrophy, 1984), 189.
4. Ibid.
5. Katherine Wolf, "Powerful Workshop," Live Orginal Farm LLC, "LO Sister: By Sadie Rob Huff," Apple App Store, Ver. 8.120.2, (2021), https://apps.apple.com/us/app/lo-sister-by-sadie-rob-huff/id1519069830.
6. Ibid.
7. Christa, "'Emet,' the Hebrew Word for Faithfulness," Christian Learning, May 28, 2021, https://www.christianlearning.com/emet-the-hebrew-word-of-faithfulness/.
8. Ibid.
9. Ibid.
10. "Faithful," BibleProject, February 9, 2021, https://bibleproject.com/explore/video/faithful/.
11. Ibid.
12. Lauren Daigle, "Lauren Daigle: God Showed Me My Future," *Guideposts*, https://guideposts.org/positive-living/entertainment/music/lauren-daigle-god-showed-me-my-future/.
13. Lana Sweeten-Shults, "Illness, 'No' on 'American Idol,' Didn't Stop Daigle," *GCU News*, September 25, 2019, https://news.gcu.edu/gcu-news/lauren-daigle-concert-grand-canyon-university/.
14. "Georgia Cross Country Champion Kathryn Foreman Lends a Hand to Those in Need," *USA Today High School Sports*, March 6,

2014, https://usatodayhss.com/2014/georgia-cross-country-
champion-kathryn-foreman-lends-a-hand-to-those-in-need.

CHAPTER 5: WHEN YOU DON'T WANT
THE STORY GOD IS WRITING

1. C. S. Lewis, *The Problem of Pain* (New York: HarperCollins, 1940).
2. Dallas Willard, *Renovation of the Heart: Putting on the Character of Christ* (Colorado Springs: NavPress, 2021), 102.
3. Ibid., 105.
4. Frank Charles Laubach, *Man of Prayer: Selected Writings of a World Missionary* (Syracuse, NY: Laubach Literacy International, 1990), 154.
5. Bob Goff, *Undistracted: Capture Your Purpose. Rediscover Your Joy* (Nashville: Nelson Books, 2022), 27–28.
6. "Passion 2018—Christine Caine," Passion, January 8, 2018, video, https://www.youtube.com/watch?v=lb5LLKQQJcE.

CHAPTER 6: YOUR IDENTITY BEYOND YOUR FEELINGS

1. Dallas Willard, *Renovation of the Heart: Putting on the Character of Christ* (Colorado Springs: NavPress, 2021), 228.
2. Ibid.
3. Sadie Robertson Huff, *Who Are You Following?: Pursuing Jesus in a Social-Media Obsessed World* (Nashville: W Publishing, 2022), 175.
4. Willard, *Renovation of the Heart*, 229.
5. Stephen R. Covey, *The 7 Habits of Highly Effective People* (New York: Simon & Schuster, 2020), 77.

CHAPTER 7: CELEBRATION IS A CALLING

1. Dawn Chere Wilkerson, "This Must Be the Place," *The Grove Podcast*, season 4, episode 13, May 4, 2022, https://podcasts.apple.com/us/podcast/this-must-be-the-place-dawncher%C3%A9-wilkerson/id1441017228?i=1000559564944.
2. Stephen R. Covey, *The 7 Habits of Highly Effective People* (New York: Simon & Schuster, 2020), 77.

3. Ibid., 348.

4. *The Jesus Bible* (Grand Rapids: Zondervan, 2016), 1860.

5. Covey, *The 7 Habits of Highly Effective People.*

CHAPTER 8: BREATHING DREAMS LIKE AIR

1. F. Scott Fitzgerald, *The Great Gatsby* (New York: Scribner, 2004), 161.

2. Louie Giglio, *Breath on a Page: Why the Word of God Is the Way of Life*, sermon series digital download, Passion Resources, https://passionresources.com/products/breath-on-a-page-louie-giglio-digital-download.

3. Firm Staff, "Ruach and the Hebrew Word for the Holy Spirt," *FIRM*, June 12, 2021, https://firmisrael.org/learn/the-hebrew-word-ruach-and-gods-breath-in-our-lungs/.

4. Ibid.

CHAPTER 9: EYES FIXED

1. David W. Chapman, "Notes on Hebrews," *English Standard Version Study Bible* (Wheaton, IL: Crossway, 2008), 2384.

CHAPTER 10: WHEN IT FEELS LIKE THINGS CAN'T GET MUCH WORSE

1. C. S. Lewis, *A Grief Observed*, ed. Douglas H. Gresham (New York: HarperCollins, 1994), xxvi.

2. Ibid., 26.

3. Ibid., 43.

4. Ibid., xxvi.

5. Lysa TerKeurst, *It's Not Supposed to Be This Way: Finding Unexpected Strength When Disappointment Leaves You Shattered* (Nashville: Thomas Nelson, 2018).

6. C. S. Lewis, *The Last Battle* (New York: HarperTrophy, 1984), 189.

Everyone thinks you've got it together.
But inside, you're asking, "Am I enough?"

Living freely in a culture of comparison

Seated with Christ is for anyone tired of comparing, competing, and clamoring for acceptance. In elegant, vulnerable prose, English lecturer Heather Holleman unveils the wonder of our being seated with Christ in the heavens (Eph. 2:6). This reflective journey into Scripture inspires us to live as we were meant to: freely and securely.

Also available as an eBook

Finding your true value and purpose begins with a simple but profound truth: *you have been wonderfully made.*